NO BRONZE STATUE

NO BRONZE STATUE

A Living Documentary of the Mildmay Mission Hospital

PHYLLIS THOMPSON

KINGSWAY PUBLICATIONS
EASTBOURNE

First published by Word Books, London 1972
This edition first published 1982

ISBN 0 86065 187 8

Front cover design by Vic Mitchell

Printed in Great Britain for
KINGSWAY PUBLICATIONS LTD
Lottbridge Drove, Eastbourne, E. Sussex BN23 6NT by
Richard Clay (The Chaucer Press) Ltd, Bungay, Suffolk

CONTENTS

FOREWORD

by Professor Sir Norman Anderson, O.B.E., LL.D., F.B.A.

Must every work of God be recorded in print, often enough by those who, however worthy, have no special aptitude for the task? And is not the history of a small mission hospital in Shoreditch very likely to fall under this implied condemnation? But here, in point of fact, is a story eminently worth telling, told by one who certainly has the ability to make that story come alive.

It starts with a vivid picture of the penury, squalor and degradation of the East End of London a century ago, in stark contrast to the cosetted life in those affluent and highly respectable homes from which a company of young women, brought up in the idle luxury of Victorian 'gentlewomen', caught anew the vision of sacrificial service. There were two factors which brought this need and these women together: the outbreak of an epidemic of cholera, on the one hand, and the beginning of a rigorous course of training for nurses intending to work in medical missions, on the other. The result was a hospital which has combined, in a unique way, a service of love and medical skill to the people of the East End with an almost incredibly long roll of honour of doctors and nurses who have found their way to every quarter of the globe.

The history of this hospital down the years has – not surprisingly – been a long battle of faith. In the early days there was the recurrent problem of where the necessary funds were to come from. More recently, there has been what at first seemed the insoluble problem of how a small hospital could survive in a day when only larger institutions commonly remain viable (especially for the training of nurses) and how the spiritual message and standards of the Mildmay could be retained when it became an insignificant cog in a Health Service financed and controlled by the State.

The men and women concerned in this history were 'of like passions' with the rest of us. The leaders who had to grapple with the problems had to fight against doubt, uncertainty and depression, while many young nurses from wealthy homes found that the seemingly endless succession of menial tasks which then fell to the lot of the new probationer drove them not only to tears but to near despair – only to be comforted and encouraged, maybe, by the inimitable Percy, who occasionally interpreted the duties of a porter in a somewhat unorthodox way. Sometimes, indeed, both leaders and nurses were at their wits' end about the future. But God was not deaf to their prayers, nor unmindful of their 'labour of love' – and both they and the Mildmay won through. Phyllis Thompson makes the whole story, and the men and women who brought it into being, come alive. This little book is, indeed, virtually their collective biography, written in the modern style: not a record of archangels and stained glass saints, but of men and women in whose footsteps ordinary people, like you and me, can aspire to follow.

Without the loving care for the sick, whoever they might chance to be, which has always been so characteristic of the Mildmay, the texts inscribed on the walls, and the daily prayers in the wards, would have seemed a hollow sham. But without the spiritual ministry which is such an integral part of the work, the loving service would have remained inarticulated and unexplained. Here is a message for us all. This book will not only hold the reader's interest but will enrich his life. It is a privilege to be asked to commend it.

But why should the task of writing a Foreword fall to me? Why indeed? I can only surmise that there were several factors which, in aggregate, prompted the invitation. First, the present Medical Superintendent, Dr. Kenneth Buxton, has been an almost lifelong friend, ever since we were exact contemporaries at Trinity College, Cambridge. Next, my wife has for some years been President of the League of Friends, and closely associated with the work of the hospital. Then again, I am in complete sympathy with the objectives of the Mildmay – to bring healing to the sick and the good news of a Saviour's love to all and sundry; and I know something of the unique services it has rendered, not only to those in the East End but to multitudes of missionaries and Christian workers in need of medical help. Finally, our dearly loved son himself, some eighteen months ago, passed from one of its wards into the immediate presence of his Lord, after receiving a loving care and ceaseless attention such as could not have been equalled, I believe, anywhere else. He had steadfastly and consistently refused any "bought" medicine, but no money could have bought better. So I write from at least a modicum of personal experience.

But the battle has not ceased, and pressing problems still confront the hospital – chief among them, perhaps, the choice of staff, possessed of all the necessary medical qualifications, dedicated to the service of the Saviour whom the Mildmay exists to proclaim and willing to pay the price of carrying the work forward in the years to come. And an essential part of that price is prayer – in which we may all join.

NORMAN ANDERSON

Chapter One

ENCOUNTER IN THE O.P.D.

I was sitting in the hospital out-patients department, resigned to a long wait before my turn came to see the doctor. The book I had brought to wile away the time successfully transported me from London's East End, with its continuous roar of traffic and its drab streets, to the awe-inspiring jungle-covered mountains of south-east Asia, and it was with quite a shock that I looked up to give my eyes and my mind a rest, and saw where I was.

The pale green walls, the softly shining wood floor, the sturdy benches, were clean but prosaic. The out-patients looked respectable but dull. The days when ragged clothing and heart-rending evidences of poverty and crime characterised the people who came to the Mildmay Mission Hospital had passed completely with the coming in of the Welfare State. If Bill Sykes and Jack the Ripper, Little Nell and Oliver Twist had their modern counterparts, there was nothing to show for it. I was about to turn back to my book when I saw a woman come through the swing doors and walk slowly in.

There was nothing to distinguish her from the other women in the large, airy room, for she was of medium height, neatly but inconspicuously dressed. It was the expression on her face that arrested me. Undisguised astonishment was mingled with awe. She looked first at one side and then at the other, reading the words that were painted on the walls, as she walked hesitantly along between the rows of benches.

Then she caught my eye. She looked so nervous and bewildered that I wanted to reassure her. 'Probably afraid of what the doctor's going to tell her,' I thought, as I smiled encouragingly at her. There was no change in her expression, but she made straight for me and sat down.

'First time I've been here,' she said, her eyes still wandering to the walls. Then she added, 'I've never been to a place like this before'.

I knew what made her say that. It was not that the O.P.D. differed so greatly in airiness and cleanliness from that of many other hospitals in the metropolis. It was the writing on the wall that made the difference.

Some people thought they ought not to be there, those texts from the Bible. A hospital wasn't the place for Biblical sayings, they said – they ought to be kept to the churches. Others thought that one here and there was all right, but one on nearly every wall was overdoing it. But there were those who asserted that this hospital existed not only to heal the sick, but to diffuse the Christian message, and texts on the wall was one way of diffusing it. There they were, and if most people ignored them, they had evidently made an impression on this visitor. Whether favourable or unfavourable I could not discern, and I wondered whether I ought to proceed cautiously. Experience having taught me, however, that when I am cautious I usually do not proceed, in the split second in which a decision had to be made I took a deep breath like a diver poised over the deep end, and said,

'Oh, it's a Christian hospital. Very nice place to be in. The doctors and nurses here are believers in the Lord Jesus Christ.' Then I went on firmly, 'They're "born again" as the Bible says'.

It was evident now, my evangelical position, and I

braced myself for the consequences of the disclosure. I was prepared for a polite withdrawal – or an irritated retort – or an argument – or a look of blank surprise. What I was not prepared for was the response she gave. Without any change of expression she said,

'Something happened to me last July. I got saved.'

'You were saved?' I ejaculated, and tried to suppress my look of surprise with a bright smile. Did she mean what I meant by being saved, I wondered, though I did not say so. But she left me in no doubt.

'I gave my heart to Jesus,' she said simply. Her eyes softened, and a smile spread over her face. I smiled back and nodded.

'I did, too, many years ago,' I said, and after that there were no problems of communication. We both felt completely at home with each other. We exchanged names but,

'Call me Lilian,' she said, and needed no persuasion to relate the incidents that led up to what happened to her last July.

Once more I forgot where I was as I listened to her story.

'When I stood in that divorce court with my hand on the Bible, I felt sort of numb,' she commenced. A married woman with two children, she had become emotionally involved with the lodger, and her husband had insisted on a divorce. She could bring the action against him, and so get custody of the children.

'Take the kids and get out!' he said angrily. He was sick of the whole affair, and whatever pangs he may have felt, kept them to himself. So Lilian, over-wrought and bewildered, agreed to say nothing about the lodger and her association with him, but to tell a few lies about cruelty instead.

It was not until a week before the case was due to come up that she knew she would be required in court to put her hand on the Bible and vow to tell the truth. The knowledge threw her into a panic, but there seemed no escape now. Unless the divorce went through and she married the lodger, she and the boys would be homeless.

The divorce was granted without question. It was all over in a few minutes, and she went to bed that night with a strange new sense of guilt. She had put her hand on the Bible and vowed to tell the truth, and had told lies. She felt as though a gigantic invisible sword was poised over her head, and sooner or later it would fall.

In the fulness of time she married the lodger, and the second marriage was no happier than the first had been. 'I didn't want to marry you,' he told her once, in a cold anger. 'You forced me into the position – I had no option.' The shock of it went deep, and added to the sullen expressions on the faces of her two young sons, revealing too clearly the fact that they were not happy, brought her to the verge of a breakdown. Then one of them left home, leaving no word as to where he had gone, and she felt she could stand it no longer. She went to the doctor and told him her misery, pouring out the whole story, including the lies told with her hand on the Bible.

'There's nothing you can do about it now,' he told her. 'You'd better just forget about it.' He gave her some medicine, and warned her that if she did not pull herself together she would be in a mental hospital within ten weeks.

She took the medicine, but she could not pull herself together, and so it came about that one Saturday afternoon, in the market where she had gone to do the weekend shopping, she stood on the pavement with the noisy crowds jostling past her, tears trickling down her cheeks, and wishing she could die.

'I just don't want to go on living,' she thought. 'Just

want to stop living . . .'

Then she saw the Bibles.

They were spread out on a trestle table next to the greengrocer's stall, and her eyes rivetted on them. So simple they looked, making no sort of a show, just the words HOLY BIBLE on their covers. And behind the stall was a man wearing a clerical collar. Bibles and a Reverend!

Something urged her to move towards him.

'I felt I had to come and speak to you,' she said, half laughing, half crying. 'I don't know why I've come. I had to come . . .'

The man looked at her, and said quietly, 'You're in trouble, aren't you? I know someone who can help you.' Then he added, rather deliberately, 'Jesus can help you'.

'Oh, I don't know anything about that,' replied Lilian impatiently. She was turning away when the man suggested that if she came to see him he could explain to her how Jesus could help her. She took the card he handed to her, and went home.

Days passed before she could make up her mind, but at last, one evening, she went to the address on the card, and found herself standing outside a front door that opened wide at her knock.

'Come in,' said the man as he grasped her hand warmly. He ushered her into a room where two men rose courteously as she entered, and introduced them.

'Please sit down,' he said. She looked round the unfamiliar room, at the kindly faces of the men, and a sense of shame deeper than anything she had ever known swept over her.

'Oh, I can't sit down here – I'm not clean enough!' she ejaculated, and then seeing their expressions of surprise, continued,

'You don't know what I'm like,' and started to tell

them. The whole sordid story came out – the deceptions, the stormy scenes, the break up of the marriage, and particularly that terrible time when she had offended God, the unseen Being whose Book was the Holy Bible. The sword of judgement seemed to tremble in the air above her, gripped by an invisible hand, ready to strike at last.

The men listened quietly until she had finished, and they looked neither shocked nor dismayed. Then the man who had stood at the Bible stall in the market place did as he had said. He told her how Jesus could help her.

She had heard of Jesus? Well, she knew He had been born in a manger and had died on a cross. He had been crucified – that was about all she knew, said Lilian.

He had died on that cross for her sins, the man explained. He had not died for His own sins, for He had none. He had died for the sins of the whole world, including hers, and because of that everything she had done wrong could be forgiven. Was she willing to kneel down, here and now, and ask Him to forgive her?

Yes, she was willing. She knelt down, and they knelt with her, and they prayed, and she prayed, asking God to forgive her.

All this she told me, somewhat incoherently, as we sat together in the hospital out-patients department. As she talked words kept coming to my mind that Lilian had probably never heard.

'I fled Him down the nights and down the days,
I fled Him down the arches of the years,
I fled Him down the labyrinthine ways
Of my own mind; and in the mist of tears,
I hid from Him . . .
From those strong Feet that followed, followed after.'

I looked at her, waiting for her to continue, for she had

come to a halt at this point, as though this concluded her story. But I was not satisfied. I wanted to know just how those strong Feet had caught up with her at last.

'What happened then?' I asked, and she went on,

'Well, then I went home. And as I was walking along the road it was as though a sword fell. As though it fell behind me. I felt as though something had cut off all those things of the past. They had gone. They weren't there to worry me any more. All those sins had gone. It was wonderful,' she said. 'I was free! free!'

When she got home she told her husband about it, and he thought she was out of her mind. 'You've gone crazy, Lilian, that's what's the matter with you,' he said. Well, if she was crazy she'd been crazy for more than half a year now, and she didn't want to change! No, she said, in answer to my question, it wasn't that her marriage was any happier. No, her son had disappeared, and she still did not know where he was. Furthermore, she was suffer- a lot of pain, and thought she might have to undergo a serious operation. That was why she had come here this evening – her doctor had put her in touch with Dr Buxton. No, life hadn't changed at all, and circumstances were no easier than they had been a year ago.

'But I've got Jesus with me now. He makes all the difference. I couldn't do without him, not for a minute – not for a moment.'

It was my first visit to the Mildmay Mission Hospital, and the place itself seemed strangely in keeping with Lilian's story. It looked so ordinary on the outside, like she did. Its garnet-coloured brick walls and heavily framed windows were just like many other buildings in the neighbourhood. Inside, the colour-washed walls, the paraphernalia of steel trolleys and oxygen drums and X-ray machines were the same as in any other hospital.

The staff uniforms were the same, too. Only the texts on the walls gave evidence that there was something distinctive about this tiny hospital.

That it was a tiny hospital could not be denied. Of the hundreds in London it ranked among the smallest, for it had only fifty-odd beds at the time, and a Government Commission had reported that no hospital with less than 200 was economic. The request for permission to build an extension looked like being refused. It would be uneconomic to spend more money on it.

'But this is the hospital that patients want to come to – some of them from the ends of the earth!' the Chairman of the Central Group Hospital Management Committee had protested. 'This is the hospital that has a waiting list for nurses, this is the hospital that has already provided a considerable sum towards the cost of its own extension!' Lord Stonham was his name, and he was a descendant of the Huguenots who had fled from the religious persecution of Protestants in France centuries before, to introduce their weaving and lace-making skills in England, and plant mulberry trees in London's East End.

'This place is doing the sort of work my ancestors used to do,' he had said when he visited the hospital. He set about making his investigations by going round the wards and asking all the patients why they had come to this particular hospital.

'I came because I wanted to come. I asked to be sent here,' were the answers he received. He asked about student nurses, and was shown a long waiting list, at a time when many other hospitals were bemoaning the shortage. He kept an eye on the accounts, and knew just how much was on the credit side of the Free Moneys Fund. It was in the region of £45,000. When the matter came up of whether little Mildmay be granted permission to build an extension, he produced his evidence with considerable eloquence. It was one of the factors that won the day in a period of crisis that was one of the biggest in the life of the hospital.

Not that Lillian and I know anything about this, of course. The thought of a hospital having crises, and sometimes having to fight for its life, does not cross my mind until years later, when I am asked to write a book about it, and begin to look into the matter. All we know, when we find ourselves in adjacent beds in Tankerville ward is that everything seems to run very smoothly, that there is a friendly family atmosphere pervading the place, and that the young nurses who tend us do so with a kindness that we find quite affecting.

'Angels – that's what they are!' we agree in an undertone to each other, as we secretly observe them. We marvel at their patience with the querulous, and their speed in hurrying towards the beds from which come agonised calls, 'Nurse! I think I'm going to be sick!' We soon get to know those who can be relied on to do the less pleasant jobs with a sympathetic smile, and our eyes scan the ward anxiously when we are in need. They are the ones we want when the irresistible claims of nature bring blushes to our cheeks, and our self-respect hangs in tatters. We have seen the words, 'Jesus was moved with compassion', on the wall in the out-patients department, but it is the feel of a strong young arm supporting our weakness, and the cheerful assurance that it is time to change the sheets anyway, easing our sense of shame, that brings the words to life.

Leaning back like queens against our carefully propped up pillows, we survey the daily pageant with satisfaction. We watch them moving up and down the ward, the young student nurses, pushing shining steel trolleys laden with flowers for our bedside tables . . . with medicines for us to swallow . . . with food for us to eat . . . with bowls of water for us to wash. . . . The trolleys move up and down the whole day, it seems. There is always something going on. And the youthful figures behind them, with their crisp clean uniforms and their stiffly starched caps perched like haloes on their heads, nod and smile as they come to our beds, making us feel more like queens than ever. 'Angels!' we breathe.

After breakfast and after visiting time in the evening, the trolleys come to a standstill with an almost magical timing, and we subside into respectful silence.

'It's time for the ward service – you're allowed to stay if you don't talk,' we whisper to our visitors. The 'Mums' whose families come to visit them evening after evening quell the restive with a warning flash of the eye. The family system of the East End is clearly matriarchal, I observe.

A firm young voice from the end of the ward announces a hymn, while hymn-books are distributed to patients and visitors. One of the angels strikes up the tune on the piano, and we sing.

'Now let us pray,' says the firm young voice, and we close our eyes while the nurse who but ten minutes ago was hurrying down the ward with a flat steel pan discreetly covered with a white cloth, addresses herself to the invisible God. Then, her smile belying the fact that there is a sinking feeling in her tummy and that her hands are cold and sticky, she says,

'A thought for us all . . . ' and goes on to speak of the changes in life's pattern, changes that none of us can avoid. Then she asserts that there is something that never changes – God's love for us. She speaks of the cross where Jesus died.

We who are patients listen attentively, but not so all

the visitors. Some of them look bored. A well-dressed woman glances at her companion with an expression of impatience. There is a background noise of the clicking of heels along the floor, the banging of a door . . .

The determined little voice continues. There is something that must be said, whether her listeners are indifferent or not. Few of them realise that a message is being delivered which lies at the heart of the hospital, and that if that message failed to be delivered the whole character of the place would change. Few of them realise that were it not for that message, and the compelling 'must' that lies behind its deliverance, there would never have been a hospital here at all.

The bells chime out from Shoreditch parish church, and the white marble-like spire gleams in the fading light, beautiful and ethereal as an aspiring thought reaching upward from an earth-bound mind. The bells chimed and the spire gleamed just the same more than a hundred years ago, when behind the church sprawled a vast huddle of verminous, broken-down buildings and filthy unswept alleys, where lived some 10,000 human beings in conditions not so very much better than those that prevail in the slums of Bombay or Calcutta today.

It was into that evil-smelling huddle, where an epidemic of cholera had broken out, that one day in 1866 two young women, clad in crinolines and bonnets, picked their way carefully over the refuse. The Victorian counterparts of the modern 'angels in the wards', they were to lay the invisible foundation of the community hospital now known as the Mildmay Mission Hospital.

No one knows their names – somehow, they were not put on record.

Chapter Two

MAKING HISTORY

The two inconspicuously dressed young women who stepped into the gloom of the Bethnal Green slums that day in 1866 had travelled less than five geographical miles to do so, but for them it was like entering another world. They came from the stratum of Victorian society that lived in large solid houses or country mansions, where capped and aproned maid-servants did the housework, where a man and a boy tended the gardens and were always on hand to take the horse and trap round to the stables when the daughter of the house returned from a drive. Their governesses had taught them how nice little girls should always be seen to the best advantage, while being heard only if called upon to sing in the drawing room where mama and papa had visitors.

In this environment they would almost certainly have lived until suitably married to admirable young men with good incomes if possible, but failing that at least with good prospects, remaining in submissive if unsatisfied seclusion had it not been for Catherine Pennefather.

Catherine Pennefather was the daughter of an English admiral and she had married the Reverend William Pennefather, son of an Irish judge. Unsatisfied seclusion was not her idea of fulfilling her destiny, and even less was it her husband's idea. They had both been born for something much more dynamic than that, and the normal round of activities of a parish could not contain them.

The Crimean War with its aftermath of fatherless children got them involved in the education of orphans. The poverty in industrial areas drew them into doing relief work. News of the American evangelist Moody, and what happened when he preached in his own country inspired them to invite him to come and preach in theirs. Meeting Christians of other denominations with identical faith and identical aims to their own, convinced them that all were 'one in Christ Jesus', and their conviction ultimately found expression in what is now the annual event of the Keswick Convention. There was so much to do, and so much needing to be done that the Pennefathers found they were always on the go, carried along by a force stronger than themselves.

That force carried them, as earlier it had carried Florence Nightingale, to Kaiserwerth in Germany. There a Lutheran pastor had established what amounted to the Protestant equivalent of a Roman Catholic convent, where single women who desired to invest their lives in service to God and humanity were helped to do so. They received plenty of experience in the Christian virtues of humility and patience by living together at close quarters. They were trained in all sorts of practical skills, including nursing. Their lives were firmly disciplined, but they seemed to thrive on it.

Seeing them made the Pennefathers think of their own countrywomen, so many of whom were idling their time away on trifles. Couldn't something like what they saw in Kaiserwerth be started in England? Couldn't an outlet be found for the energies and abilities of women who were unhappily quenching the urge to be up and doing in an England where the social conscience was awakening at last?

For the social conscience was being deeply stirred. The

novels of Charles Dickens had played their part in that stirring, just as *Uncle Tom's Cabin* had aroused such a sense of shame and indignation that the abolition of slavery in America had been hastened on by its publication. Knowledge of the squalor of the slums of the great cities, where drunkenness and lewdness were the order of the day, and a street fight drew a ragged dirty crowd yelling with glee from the alleys and tenements around, 'like a human sewer suddenly discharging its contents', was beginning to penetrate like a bad odour into the homes of the well-to-do. Florence Nightingale's fearless disclosures of conditions in the British Army in the Crimea had added to the general uneasiness. Evangelical Christians particularly were being forced to examine themselves in the light of the Good Samaritan. Were they, in fact, like the priest and the Levite, 'passing by on the other side'?

One way and another, the Pennefathers felt the time was ripe. Now was the opportunity to form a little team of Christian women who could care for orphans, teach the illiterate to read, nurse the sick, and generally go about doing good, like their Master.

There was a lot that women could not do, of course. It was the men who must do the public speaking, go into Parliament, become doctors, and administer justice. But Florence Nightingale, heroine of the public, had made it evident that there were some things women could do that men could not. Above all, as far as the Pennefathers were concerned, there was the example of the deaconesses from Kaiserwerth, Protestant Sisters of Charity as Elizabeth Fry had described them. Not only were they diffusing the Good News of the Kingdom of God by deed as well as word in their own country, but they had established institutions in other lands as well. Here were women doing a woman's job, not as isolated individuals who could be regarded as oddities, but as members of a community with a distinctive uniform and a status in society. If in Germany, why not in England, asked the Pennefathers.

As was their custom, they put the question to God a long time before they put it to man. They proceeded cautiously with what might have been regarded as a new idea – had not the deaconesses of the Early Church provided them with a convincing argument that it was really nothing more than a resuscitation of an old one. In 1857 'The Association of Female Workers' was formed, with Catherine Pennefather as the President, and in 1860 the Missionary Training Home for Young Women was opened. It was the first of its kind in England. In 1864 the Pennefathers moved from Barnet to Mildmay Park, a rather dreary suburb on the border of the East End of London, and the young women moved with them, to become the Mildmay Deaconesses – a name that was to stick for half a century.

Day after day the young women emerged from their Deaconess Home next door to the Mildmay Conference Centre, to visit the poor and the sick, instruct the uneducated, lead classes and meetings, and generally make themselves useful where they were needed. Evening after evening they returned. On entering the hall they moved back into position their name plates to announce that they were in (telegraph boys were soon on the run if they did not return on time), had their supper and went to bed. Never, on any account, were any of them out alone later than 10.30 p.m.

They received no salary, of course, those young ladies. On the contrary, they were expected to make a contribution towards the upkeep of the Home.

Breakfast was the family meal, when they all gathered round the long table, standing behind their chairs as each one repeated by heart a Scripture text. The delinquent who overslept, leaving no time to memorise her text, blushed before the reproachful eye of the Lady Superintendent who never failed to repeat one herself, word perfect and often quite long. After breakfast news was shared, and letters read aloud from the few deaconesses who had already gone abroad as missionaries. Deeply moved were the young ladies sitting round the well-laden Victorian breakfast table by the accounts of the poverty, the misery and the heathen darkness of the lands from which those letters were written. They saw plenty of poverty in the course of their visitations, but it was probably not until the vicar of St Philip's, Bethnal Green, sent his plea for help to the Pennefathers, that it began to dawn on them just how much misery and heathen darkness was flourishing on their own doorstep.

It was not so much because of the poverty and the misery and the heathen darkness that the vicar of St Philip's wrote, however, because all that had existed for a long time, and to him, poor man, it no longer made news. But now another woe had been added. Morning after morning the death cart rumbled over the cobbled streets to collect the bodies of those who had died in the night. The stench was sickening. People were dying like flies.

Cholera had broken out. And in his desperation the vicar wrote to the Pennefathers to ask if any of the Mildmay deaconesses could come to help in this terrible crisis.

We do not know what were the first reactions of the Pennefathers, and then of the deaconesses themselves, to this request. No intimate records of those early days exist, and in any case it was not the fashion to admit to feelings of distaste or fear in the mid-nineteenth century. Only sentiments that were noble were to be expressed. But Bethnal Green was in the slums! The slums!

The deaconesses already had more than enough work to do among what the Victorians termed 'the deserving poor'. The orphans and the widows, the cottagers eking out a living on a pittance, the workmen and their families who had had no chance to learn to read and write, the factory workers, the servant girls who had nowhere to go when they had a few hours' freedom, the sick people who were left alone in hovels for hours on end because those who could work had to go and earn the bread – all these branches of society were claiming the attention of the deaconesses, and the Pennefathers might well have argued that they already had their hands full.

Furthermore, these young ladies with a genteel upbringing were already exposing themselves to dangers of disease, tuberculosis and the like, as they moved about among the poor. But to expose them to cholera, from which they might die an agonising death within twenty-four hours! Was it right to do that?

And to let them go to the slums! It was in the slums that the thieves and the robbers lived, in the slums that drunken men lurched from the gin palaces to fight in the streets, where unkempt women threw refuse out of the windows, and emerged at twilight, scarlet-lipped and hard-eyed, to stand at street corners or walk up and down on their pavement beats. Even the pathetic, whining urchins in their tattered trousers were known to beg with one hand and pick your pocket with the other. They were taught to do it! The slums were not merely places of poverty, they were the home of the criminal and 'the fallen woman'. And the question had to be decided – was it right to let the undefended young deaconesses go there?

Whatever may have been the discussions and the weighing of pros and cons that preceded the final decision can only be surmised. Nor do we know what criticism had to be faced when it became known that 'the Pennefathers have sent two young ladies, alone, into the slums of Bethnal Green'. A year before, thirty-year-old Hudson Taylor, whose home was in Pyrland Road just round the corner from Mildmay Park, had set out with a group of enthusiastic young people to evangelise inland China – and in that group were some unmarried ladies, in their very early twenties! It was criminal! Side whiskers bristled and bosoms heaved in Victorian drawing-rooms as the verdict was passed that it ought not to be allowed – something ought to be done to stop it.

The Pennefathers knew all about the criticism, and asserted with Hudson Taylor that since it was God Who had called those young ladies to serve Him in China, He would be the One responsible for them. When the matter of the cholera epidemic came up they stuck to it that the same thing applied to any Mildmay deaconesses who might go into the slums of Bethnal Green.

The outcome of the plea from the vicar of St Philip's, therefore, was the speedy preparation of a little property in the heart of the slum to serve as a base for the deaconesses. Then two of them set off one morning to do what they could by faith in God, and the use of such medical skill as they had acquired, to stay the plague.

How much medical skill they had acquired, of course, is open to conjecture. Florence Nightingale was still fighting her long battle to change public opinion about nursing. Women employed as hospital nurses were still likely to be those who could get no other work, and who were encouraged to do the more unpleasant tasks, like laying out the body, by the promise of a little extra gin. Any medical skill the deaconesses might have learned would certainly not have been gained in hospitals – more likely it was picked up from the time-honoured habits of their childhood nannies. At any rate, there was now one famous textbook to which they could apply. Miss Florence Nightingale had published *Notes on Nursing* some seven years before, and any young lady who had studied it thoroughly could be assured that she was well qualified to take charge in a sick-room. And since, in the Mildmay Deaconess home, diligent study and efficiency in any subject tackled were insisted on, no one could question their right to do medical work in the slums.

So off they set, one day in 1866, in their crinolines and capes, travelling on the North London Railway to Shoreditch Station, to walk from there to their assignment. They made history that day, those two young women, trying not to be either apprehensive or self-conscious at the stares of the slum-dwellers as they picked their way along the bustling market in Petticoat Lane. They made history – yet no one even knows their names!

No one knows how they fared in their fight against cholera, either. All that is known is that when eventually the epidemic had burnt itself out, and the death cart no longer rumbled along collecting bodies every morning, the deaconesses continued to go every day to Bethnal Green. And it was decided that one of them should live there altogether, while others went daily to help her with the meetings, and the visiting, and the clinics and the soup kitchens, and all the various activities that were on foot.

For the fact is, the deaconesses took to the slums, and the slums took to the deaconesses. It was not long before the young ladies could go singly along alleys and into squalid courtyards where policemen on their beat only dared to go in pairs. 'Angels – that's wot they are,' said Bethnal Green, approving their deeds if largely indifferent to their doctrines. As for the deaconesses, they emerged from those gloomy caverns of rat-ridden old houses with the most moving stories of what they found there.

It was not only the poverty and the misery that affected them so deeply, the little children left alone with only a raw potato to chew, the dying baby being given gin out of a broken bottle by its tipsy mother, and the like. It was the dogged, plucky, loving spirit in many of the families they found there that touched them, too. Lousy-headed little boys and girls would swarm around when there was a free meal going, but they dragged their younger brothers and sisters along as well. 'My little bruvver – give 'im some, miss!' There were men who trudged the streets all day, looking for work, willing to do anything 'to turn an honest penny' to support their families. There were women who sat up far into the night making matchboxes at two and a half pennies a gross, with nothing to eat but what was left over from the children's meal. The way these East End families stuck together! And the way they loved their animals!

'You see, ma'am, there are ten of us to keep,' explained one woman, wife of a coster monger, who had been working all day making matchboxes, and had earned about ten pence. 'There's me and me 'usband and the six children and the two donkeys . . . ' One of the donkeys was too old to work now, but 'We couldn't let 'er starve, ma'am, now could we?' So that made ten mouths to feed, and if the old donkey went hungry sometimes, it was only because the family was going hungry, too.

Naturally, the deaconesses could not help talking about what they saw and heard. When they got back to the Deaconess Home, they talked. When they went to speak at meetings for working men, meetings for servant girls, meetings for mothers and meetings for children, they talked. When they went on visits to their friends and relations, back to the comfortable homes where they reverted for a time to a life in which they did no dirty work and had plenty of time to entertain visitors, they talked. They told of the poverty, and of those who exploited it, enticing hard-earned money out of pockets with the promise, 'drunk for a copper, dead drunk for two!' outside the public houses; of the wives whose teeth were knocked out and eyes bruised, of terrified, shivering, hungry little children; and of poor people who got ill and died just because they could not afford to buy some medicine.

But they had something else to say, too. They talked about the wonderful way in which they saw God working at Bethnal Green. They talked about the poor drunkard who had been so melted when he heard about Jesus dying on the cross for him, and how his life had been changed since then. They talked about women who had stopped quarrelling, and who came along to the meetings instead, and kept their poor homes clean. They told about little children waiting for an hour on the Mission doorstep, begging for stories about Jesus, some shyly confiding that they had asked Him into their hearts. Only those with a heart of stone could remain unmoved when they heard what the deaconesses had to tell, read what they had to report, and above all, see how they loved the people of Bethnal Green, and wanted to get back to them.

So it is not really surprising that when William Pennefather died in 1874 and a memorial fund was opened, it was decided that the money should be used, not to erect a bronze statue of him and put it in as prominent a place as possible, but to establish a Medical Mission hospital in the slums instead.

Catherine Pennefather was all in favour of the idea if,

in fact, it was not hers in the first place. It was just the sort of thing her husband would have wanted, she asserted, and with that dedicated enterprise of hers, set about doing things in what she considered the right order. She started with God, went on to people, and last of all, to buildings.

Tracing the beginning of anything with God is no simple matter, for it involves secret transactions between the soul and its Maker, in which no other can really share. And in the final analysis, God is always the beginning. That is certainly the way Catherine Pennefather saw it, and as far as the Mildmay Mission Hospital was concerned,

> '*. . . a Hand invisible was rearing,*
> *A new creation in the secret deep,*'

to quote from a little poem that for years appeared on the cover of the Mildmay magazine she edited.

For her the awareness of that new creation probably began in 1869, when her husband invited Dr Burns-Thompson to speak in the Mildmay Conference Hall on the subject of medical missions. Dr Burns-Thompson had started his medical career in a very unusual way when, as a young Arts student in Edinburgh, he went into one of the poorest districts of the city to evangelise by door to door visiting, and entering one house was brought to a sudden halt.

'I had scarce got into the house,' he said, 'when a sharp little Irishwoman approached me abruptly and said,

' "What do you want, sir?"

'I was not so experienced in visiting then as I am now, and the question disturbed me. Her son was lying on a low settee at the side of the room, the worse for drink. He looked up at me and cried to his mother, "Put 'im oot, mither!" But as I lingered the youth got angry and cried with an oath,

'"Mither, canna ye put 'im oot?" I was still more disturbed, and remarked to the woman, "I was just going round your district, and I thought I would look in and see you. You are not looking well."

'"Sure, and it's not well that I am," was her reply.

'"I think you would be the better of a little medicine," I said. I knew at that time no more of medicine than the man in the moon. I knew the virtue of only one drug, which I had learned in infancy, and I got a cup from her and went to the nearest druggist's and got a dose of castor oil.'

Had the woman realised he was only an arts student she might not have accepted his remedy, but she mistook him for a doctor, and swallowed it. Next time he visited her she welcomed him eagerly, willing to listen to anything he had to say to her. The medicine he had given her was wonderful, she said, it had made a new woman of her.

That dose of castor oil was the turning point in young Burns-Thompson's life. He had been planning to go to theological college in preparation for the life of a foreign missionary, but decided to take up medicine instead. If the prescription of a dose of castor oil was so successful in changing the attitude of that one Irish family towards a preacher of the Gospel, what might not be achieved through a full medical training? Burns-Thompson felt that as a means of evangelism among the poor it would be more effective than theology. That, briefly, is why he became a doctor, then the Superintendent of the Edinburgh Medical Missionary Society, and then established the first medical mission in the United Kingdom.

What he had to tell about that medical mission so gripped the Pennefathers that they decided they must go and see it for themselves. As they stood on a bridge above the Cowgate of Edinburgh it looked to them like a deep, gloomy trench with human beings swarming like ants at the bottom. In one of the narrow alleys leading off it, so dark as to be like the entrance to a mine, they found the medical mission housed in what had been a whisky shop. The patients who flocked there, thousands of them in the course of a year, 'were the pink of ungodliness, the elite of ragamuffins, outcasts, infidels', as Dr Burns-Thompson expressed it. Had he gone to them with theology neither he nor his message would have had a chance – but going to them with medicine, with healing for the body, it was a different matter. 'Now they come and sit and hear of the salvation that is without money and without price,' said Burns-Thompson exultantly.

What worked so well in the slums of Edinburgh would surely work just as well in the slums of East London, thought the Pennefathers. Even when William Pennefather died, the thought persisted in Catherine's mind. A hospital for the people of Bethnal Green. But how could you have a hospital if you hadn't a doctor? She approached Dr Burns-Thompson and asked if he would help by providing a Christian medical man if Mildmay could provide the hospital. Yes, he would do that. She went with the Superintendent of the Deaconess Home, along with a doctor and an architect, to Bethnal Green, and in the midst of the welter of ramshackle buildings and alleys, tenements and heaps of rubble, the architect spied a disused warehouse.

'There's your hospital,' he said.

The others looked at it without enthusiasm. That – a hospital? Oh yes, it could be converted into a most satisfactory hospital, he insisted, and sure enough he was right. In 1877 it was opened, a hospital with a ward for men and a ward for women and a ward for children, with a doctor, three nurses, and five Mildmay deaconesses to act as probationers.

For the next fifteen years that converted warehouse was

the Mildmay Mission Hospital. In 1880 Dr William Gauld became its first Medical Superintendent. He had worked in Cowgate with Dr Burns-Thompson, where he was known as 'the bonnie doctor', then gone to China as a missionary, and it was ill-health that brought him back to England. The ill-health did not remain, but fortunately for Bethnal Green, Dr Gauld did. The Mission Hospital was asserted by Dr Burns-Thompson to be the most thoroughly equipped medical mission in Great Britain.

'This must be a training-school!' he exclaimed, the first time he entered it. Florence Nightingale's first School of Nursing had been opened in 1860, with fifteen venturesome young women enrolled as probationers. That inspired beginning had been followed up by other schools of nursing, and Burns-Thompson, practical man of vision that he was, grasped eagerly at the opportunity for women to be trained as missionary nurses, just as men were being trained as missionary doctors. Doors fast closed to the theologian, he observed, readily opened to the medical. Let the theologian follow the medical in! Now that nursing was at last finding a place as a respected profession for women,

'The Mission Hospital at Bethnal Green must be a training school!' he said.

His enthusiasm communicated itself to Miss Coventry, Lady Superintendent of the Deaconess Home. She went to Edinburgh to see him about it. It was one thing for the young deaconesses to gain a few useful tips in the use of medicine, bandaging, and the like, to use in their evangelistic work, whether it be in China or India or Africa or Bethnal Green. It was one thing for them to assist the three experienced nurses in the hospital, taking special responsibility for the ward services, visiting patients when they went back to their homes, making the spiritual side of the work their main concern. Very well they did it, too. 'They give you a lot of religion there, but they don't stuff it down your throat,' as a woman from Bethnal Green, hop-picking in Kent, explained to someone she met there. 'They don't stuff it down your throat – they sandwich it, like . . .' But it was a different matter for them to be trained as nurses, for Dr Burns-Thompson emphasised that they must take their nursing training seriously. They must not only be good Christians, they must be good nurses, too.

'I must warn you that not every lady who might like to be trained for this service is fitted for it,' he said. 'There are some whose fingers are all thumbs, and they can never apply a bandage or a dressing tidily, however long they may be in your hands. It is a mere waste of time to keep hammering away at such cases; they can never be worked up so as to give you satisfaction. Others again, with warm, loving hearts, are sometimes so excitable that when an emergency occurs they lose their presence of mind, and stand gazing in bewilderment.'

Piety and gumption, said Burns-Thompson, were what were required in a good missionary nurse. 'Their piety must be unquestionable; but they need more. They must have gumption. They must have eyes all round their head, common sense, tact, circumspection.'

In 1883, therefore, Dr Gauld secured the voluntary services of lecturers for his nurses, and the Mission Hospital was launched as a teaching school for nurses. The only fault that Burns-Thompson could find with the whole set-up was that the hospital was really too small, with only thirty beds, and it ought to be enlarged. He had his eye on an old warehouse adjoining the hospital, but it was decided that what was really needed was an entirely new hospital, to be built for the purpose. There was a lot of going hither and thither, looking for a site, and when one was found that seemed suitable it was not in the centre of the district, but right on the edge, by the parish church at Shoreditch. It was a great pity, said some, but when, a short time later, the whole of the slum district was ordered to be demolished, and all the buildings in Turville Street, including the hospital, were included in the order, they agreed that God, Who knew ahead of time what was going to happen, had guided to the right place.

It was in 1890 that the foundation stone of the new hospital was laid by the Countess of Tankerville who, with a friend, had raised half of the money required for it. A great occasion was that stone-laying ceremony, with a great marquee erected on the site. The evangelicals connected with the Keswick movement flocked to it, their frock coats and tall hats well brushed for the occasion, their ladies in leg o' mutton sleeves, frills and feathers all more subdued than the prevailing fashion encouraged, but well dressed in comparison to the threadbare and tattered clothes of the East-enders who hovered around to see the fun.

Dr Gauld, in his report, explained some of the difficulties being encountered in running the present hospital in Turville Street. His language was more restrained than that of the journalists who reported on conditions in the neighbourhood in graphic terms, describing the open drains, the slimy unswept streets, the smells of decaying rubbish and urine, the violence, the drunkenness, the lewdness. He merely gave 'the noisy character of the street' as a reason for building the new hospital on the outskirts rather than in the centre of the notorious district. It interfered with the proper rest and sleep of both patients and nurses, he said, which retarded the recovery of the patient and broke down the health of the nurses who, it had been found, could only keep well there for about six weeks. After that they needed a change and rest, though they always hurried back again as soon as they were fit. The smells and the sights and the sounds, especially in the hot weather when everyone crowded into the streets, were so sickening and unnerving that six weeks of it was about as much as they could stand without being ill themselves.

Some people had advocated moving away from the neighbourhood altogether, and building the hospital in a quiet, healthy suburb. This suggestion had not been acted on, however, Dr Gauld explained, because it was realised that the presence of a hospital right on the doorstep and ease of access gave a sense of security to the people it was intended to serve. They would never go to it at all if it were out in a suburb. So in the environs of Bethnal Green it should remain, and the nurses would remain along with it. As a result of their labours, Dr Gauld said, literally hundreds had found Christ as their Saviour, including several Jews.

Two years later the Mildmay Mission Hospital, built in good red brick on three sides of an oblong courtyard, was completed. Five storeys high it was, the two wings like welcoming arms outstretched, and with a ward for men and a ward for women and a ward for children. There were doctors' surgeries and a nurses home, and bedrooms for the domestic staff as well, and basements. The entrance was in a cobbled alley called Austin Street, but however dirty the alley might be, the hospital courtyard was well swept and tidy, and on the occasion of the opening animated and alive with the visitors who had come to join in the joyful though solemn service of dedication.

The hospital itself was declared open by Mrs Mathieson, wife of the Treasurer of the Mildmay Trust. That same year his work had received special commendation in the *Statist* where London charities were under review. Of all the Home Missions whose accounts had been investigated, this one was declared to be the model.

'We cannot close this notice without reference to the Mildmay Mission. It is one of the largest of such societies, and has twenty-four branches of work – missions, lodging houses, homes, infirmaries, etc. Its accounts are admirably kept and are, indeed, a model for other similar societies. The whole of the money received is spent, and the committee seem content to trust to the continued support of charitable people year by year. In short, there is not a single point in which this society runs counter to our ideal of the financial management of a charity, and we wish every member of the committees of all the London charities would obtain a copy of its accounts and study them.' The writers went on to say that their judgement was perfectly unbiased. They had no knowledge of any of the institutions under review except that which they could gather from their accounts. As for their religious tenets, they were happy to wash their hands of them. 'Theology is outside our province. Funds and their application claim our whole attention.'

Mildmay was in the ascendant, and the newly-built hospital was only one of its twenty-four branches. Catherine Pennefather had planned to be present at the opening, and plant the plane tree in the courtyard, but when the time came she was unfit to go, and Miss Coventry planted it instead.

Her absence was referred to by more than one with regret – it seemed so sad that 'the mother of Mildmay' could not be with them.

'We ought to be reminded that she, though absent, is yet a very real power; a power whose source and development spring from her prayers, and from the rare gift which enables her to utilise such a variety of talent with such unexpected results. Every text on the walls of the institutions under her care speaks of the absorbing aim of her life . . . ' Her absence was a serious blank, it was reported.

But Catherine Pennefather was a wise old lady, and for all her ability, and the way she could manage people, her gifted pen and her eloquent speech, she had no very great opinion of herself. She felt they would manage very well without her. She had always liked that little excerpt from the poem about the beauty of the coral reef, and how it had come into being. For years now that excerpt had appeared in the Mildmay magazine she edited.

Each wrought alone, yet, all together wrought,
Unconscious, not unworthy instruments
By which a Hand Invisible was rearing
A new creation in the secret deep.
Omnipotence wrought in them, with them, by them,
Hence what Omnipotence alone could do,
Worms did.'

Some people may have felt it was not the best simile to use, and that a quotation about something more attractive than worms might have been found – peacocks, for instance. But for the sort of people who took a low view of themselves, and marvelled that Omnipotence should deign to work in them, with them, and by them at all, worms seemed very suitable. Omnipotence did not change, so as long as there was always an adequate supply of the right sort of worms, the new creation in the invisible depths of London's East End would continue.

Two months after the newly-built Mildmay Mission Hospital was opened, Catherine Pennefather died.

Chapter Three

MILDMAY IN THE ASCENDANT

Bethnal Green was slowly looking up. The rotting, rat-ridden slums of the Jago were being demolished and in their stead tall tenement houses were appearing, with concrete stairways and iron railings and a lavatory on nearly every floor. Roads took the place of alleys, and behind Shoreditch Church a bandstand had been erected on a high mound with paths round it, and seats (free). The London Gardens Guild had been established, too, with its aim of making London a city of flowers, and Lord Noel Buxton, its leader, was encouraging their growth in window boxes. The ragamuffins from the dark courts of the Jago wouldn't have known a daisy if they had seen one, but now green growing things in pots, called aspidistras, were making their appearance in the homes of those who aspired to a better way of life.

The gin palaces were not having it all their own way, either. No longer were they the only places where the weary could sit in a warm, convivial atmosphere, away from the dreariness of a damp, filthy, overcrowded room called 'home'. Coffee houses were appearing, mainly at the instigation of those who were on the warpath against strong drink, and Mission Halls offered rival attractions in the form of clubs and meetings, Bands of Hope and jumble sales, all with the aim of encouraging virtue and helping the needy. The dramatic change in the life of Fred Charrington, who had turned his back on the proceeds of the family's famous breweries to go to the slums preaching the Gospel and urging temperance, was reflected in the lives of other well-to-do evangelical Christians. Not only was the Salvation Army, started in 1865, waging its open war against degradation and drunkenness, to be followed by the Church Army twenty years later, but dozens of smaller, independent groups were establishing their Mission Halls cheek by jowl with the public houses. Hymn singing to the accompaniment of harmonium wafted out into the drab streets, and if it evoked a jeer then (as the memory of it often evokes a sneer now), it had its effect, drawing the crowds, influencing public opinion, and winning some to a new life.

It was going on all over London, this infiltration of hearty, practical Christianity, and the Mildmay Deaconesses were in demand north, south, east and west, to help with the clubs and the lodging-houses, the women's meetings and the soup kitchens, and to support the Temperance Movement.

The Temperance Movement may be said to have started in the eighteenth century, when John Wesley impressed on his Methodists the dangers of strong drink and advised them to avoid it altogether. It was a new idea in those days, but gradually it caught on among Christians who held similar evangelical views, and by the time the twentieth century dawned Temperance was almost an adjunct to the Gospel. A glass of port or sherry might be sipped on special occasions by independent thinkers, but by and large, 'Thank you – I don't drink', was the accepted formula.

'Even if an occasional glass wouldn't harm me, it might set a bad example to those with a weakness foı alcohol,' was a sufficiently logical explanation, when explanation was called for. Usually, however, it was not even necessary, real Christianity and total abstinence being considered to go hand in hand. This was especially so among the working classes, and it took on a militant aspect in the slums. The Temperance workers and the publicans were in opposite camps, and no one was left in any doubt about it.

There was plenty to back up the Temperance workers' insistence that drink was an enemy, and a destroyer of children. The description of a drunkard home published in an official enquiry was devastating. Broken windows stuffed with rags, floors, walls, beds filthy, the stench sickening, no food in the cupboard, and what was worse, no water, but,

'. . . on the table lies a beer can; around it half-naked children stand perplexed, pale, hungry and ill'. Their heads were alive with vermin and festering with sores, the writer reported, and continued, 'They would be in tears were they ordinary children, but tears in them have long since dried up . . . '

This sort of thing must be dealt with, it was agreed, though views on how it should be done varied. Some asserted it was a matter for legislation, and called on Parliament to introduce stricter licensing laws, while others declared it must be done through the individual. Get the individual to see the danger of strong drink, and encourage him to resist it, they said. Help him to make up his mind not to touch it! Hence the Total Abstainers Societies, the Bands of Hope, the Rechabites – and the signing of the pledge.

It was this business of signing the pledge, of coming out with an open decision to be done with the drink once and for all that was the cause of a good deal of irritated argument, especially down Hoxton way where the Hoxton Hall Mission was the centre of the Temperance movement. Many were those who didn't hold with getting drunk, but didn't hold with signing the pledge, either. There wasn't no harm in a quiet mug of beer, they asserted, and when their wives reminded them that just as one thing leads to another, so one mug had the same propensity, they stoutly affirmed that whatever other people might do, they knew where to draw the line. They weren't going to be bullied into signing no pledge just to please some parson or some deaconess, as the case might be. And if in a weak moment they had signed it, that wasn't binding. . . .

Just such an argument was going on one day in the Bower household in a terrace house near Shoreditch Church. Mrs Bower was all for the pledge and keeping it. Too much of the meagre family income went into the pockets of the local publican for her liking, what with the children always being hungry, and the fear of being turned out into the street if the rent wasn't paid promptly. Mr Bower was defiantly defending his rights, mug of beer on the table, when a step was heard on the landing and a knock at the door made husband and wife look at each other with alarm.

'It's the Deaconess!' hissed Mrs Bower. Quick as a trice Mr Bower whisked the mug off the table and deposited it underneath instead, just as the door was opening. The Deaconess entered, was greeted cordially, invited to take a seat by a genial Mr Bower, looking as innocent as a babe, and hoping fervently that the conversation would not take a turn pledge-ward.

But it did. It swung round to the subject as unerringly as the needle of a compass swings to the north.

'And are you still keeping the pledge, Mr Bower?' enquired the Deaconess with disconcerting directness. Mr Bower was cornered. He grinned sheepishly and admitted,

'No – I'm afraid not.'

'Well, then,' said the Deaconess drily, 'You might as well bring that mug of beer out from under the table, mightn't you?' There was a value in signing the pledge if it helped a man to resist temptation, but it was worse than useless if it turned him into a hypocrite. Much better to carry on their conversation with the beer mug openly displayed on the table. It probably didn't bother the Deaconess to see it there nearly as much as it now embarrassed Mr Bower!

What ensued between husband and wife later Mrs Bower did not disclose, but there can be no doubt she had scored a point.

Life was enough of a struggle for Mrs Bower without a husband's weakness for the bottle to add to it. What with the children growing out of their clothes, and babies arriving year after year, it was all she could do to keep them fed, let alone keep them clothed and shod. As for keeping them warm – well, she was glad there were the meetings in the Mildmay Hall to take them to, for it was warm there, and she was thankful for a place to go and sit and rest a bit. Even when the eighth baby arrived, a boy they called Percy, she went along whenever she could. And if she could only read a few words, she learned the hymns by heart and sang them with gusto.

It was comforting there at the Mildmay. You felt you were wanted. The young doctors who saw you when you went along to clinic smiled when they recognised you,

'Good evening, Mrs Bower!' they'd say, and ask after the baby. Real toffs they were, been to college and all, but they weren't too proud to speak to you. The nurses, too. Proper young ladies, drove around in carriages when they were at home, but you'd never know it, the way they'd sit beside you and have a homely chat. Took a real interest in you, they did, and as for looking after you when you were in hospital – well, it was like being in Heaven to be there, except for the pain. Everybody who went there said so. The nurses themselves, however, assured them that

Heaven was much, much better than Mildmay, there was simply no comparison. When they sang about it at the services in the wards and in the Mission Hall they did so with such ardour that they seemed to glow. There was no doubt but that they believed what they were singing about. The joys that awaited them in Jerusalem the Golden were reflected in their faces, and before long everyone was joining in, asserting fervently that they would all 'meet on that beautiful shore'.

No one was left in any uncertainty as to how they could do so, either. That Jesus was the way, the truth and the life was displayed in bold letters opposite the entrance gate of the hospital, and the same message was heard inside. There was no other way to the City of Gold but through faith in Jesus Who had died on the cross that we might all enter in, and the young doctors doing their houseman's year at Mildmay affirmed it constantly. They had come to the hospital, not only to heal the sick but to preach the Gospel, and if they found it a greater ordeal to face a congregation than to sit for their exams, they did it all the same. That was why they had chosen to come to the Mildmay. They wanted to start being missionaries right there, and in many cases it was their stepping off place to service overseas, in India or Africa or China.

Young Tom Bragg was one of them. He had made up his mind as a teenager to be a servant of Jesus Christ. He often told the story of how he was one day cycling along a coast road, alone, when there came to him such an overwhelming sense of the love of God that he got off his bicycle, and in the stillness of that afternoon dedicated his life to God, for however short or however long it might be. Public school and University behind him, he went to the Edinburgh Royal Infirmary for his medical training, and while there, like many another young student, visited the

Cowgate Medical Mission. It proved to be the stepping stone that led him to Mildmay to do his houseman's year. He wanted to fit himself as best he could to be a medical missionary in China, whither he planned to go with as little delay as possible.

If there was no delay for him in Mildmay, however, there was considerable distraction, all caused by hearing one of the nurses singing,

God holds the key of all unknown
And I am glad,
If other hands should hold the key
Or if He trusted it to me,
I might be sad.

A very sweet voice she had, and as it came quietly trilling along the corridor he heard it with a sudden sense of significance.

'If those words are true in her life,' he thought, 'then she is the one for me.' So he made some enquiries.

The nurse, he discovered, was Grace Josephine Wakefield, and she had come to Mildmay after being for a while in the Deaconess Home.

How she got to the Deaconess Home was a story in itself, for Grace Josephine Wakefield was a society debutante, a very gay and graceful one, not in the least the sort of girl one would have expected to find in a Deaconess Home. She had been born in New Zealand, educated in England, 'finished' in France, and was most satisfactorily launched in society when the whole course of her life was changed through hearing a man preaching on the promenade at Eastbourne.

To many of his contemporaries young Josiah Spiers was making a great fool of himself, going to the seaside during holiday time to gather the children around him on the sands, tell them Bible stories, and get them all singing sacred songs with catchy tunes. On this particular occasion, however, he was preaching to an adult audience, it being late in the evening, when well brought up children were all in bed. As for the attractive Miss Wakefield, she was on her way to a ball, and was only delayed because a large crowd had gathered to listen to the young preacher, so she and her companions, curiosity aroused, ordered the coachman to stop the carriage to see what it was all about.

It was all about salvation from sin and Jesus and eternal life. There was probably little in it that she had not heard before, one way and another, but never had she been arrested by it as now, never convinced of its reality, never realised that it had anything to do with her. The waves lapped quietly on the pebbled beach, the lights twinkled and glowed from the fashionable hotels along the front, but all receded from her consciousness as Grace Josephine Wakefield, standing there in her shimmering evening dress, agleam with her jewels, came face to face with Reality at last.

I heard His call,
'Come follow'
That was all.
Earth's joys grew dim,
My soul went after Him.
I rose and followed
That was all. . . .

In later years she must have sung that chorus often, and it summed up her case very well. She sold her jewels, turned away from the gay social life opening up before her, and deliberately set herself to find how she could best follow the One Who, though He was rich, became poor, that through His poverty others might be rich.

She applied unsuccessfully to join the Salvation Army, then the Church Army, and was eventually advised to go to the Mildmay Deaconess Home, as being the sort of place that was probably more suitable for one of her youth and upbringing. From there she was sent to the Mildmay Mission Hospital, and though there were times when she sang, there were times when she wept from sheer weariness, too. She was accustomed to the physical exertion of riding and dancing and playing tennis, but sweeping rooms and polishing furniture had not been in her line at all. As for cleaning sinks – well, her despairing tears dropped sadly into the one in the children's ward, as she scrubbed and scraped at greasy dirt that steadfastly refused to yield to soap and water. However, if she sometimes wept in private, she smiled and sang in public, and the heart of Dr Tom Bragg was won. He found a sympathetic ally in Miss Cattell, the matron. It was in her dark little private sitting room that the young couple plighted their troth, to unite their lives and their energies in establishing a hospital in north-west China, run as nearly as was possible on the lines of the one in which they had met in Bethnal Green.

It was not the first time such a thing happened at Mildmay, nor the last time, either. Mrs Bower and others like her who went along to the meetings in the Mission Hall got quite used to it, expressing their private opinions to each other as to the suitability ('Ah! Saw it coming, I did!') or otherwise ('Well! I *am* surprised'), of the various romances. It was all the outcome of the community spirit that pervaded the place, where everybody knew everybody else's business, and felt they had a right to. The top hat and smock coat of Doctor Gauld made him as familiar a sight to the people of Bethnal Green and those down Shoreditch way as any hunting squire was to his villagers, and no 'lady of the manor' commanded more respect than the gentle-faced, dignified Miss Cattell in her high necked blouses and long straight skirts with only the hint of a bustle. They reigned in their respective spheres for periods that spanned thirty years in his case and nearly a quarter of a century in hers. By the time he retired, in 1913, the Mildmay Hospital had become one of the landmarks of the neighbourhood, and as for its influence abroad, the records told that thirty-five doctors and nearly one hundred nurses, twenty-four of whom were fully qualified, had gone to the mission field.

Mildmay institutions and missions generally, as listed in the annual reports, numbered nearly thirty. Things were apparently continuing as usual. If there were ominous signs, here and there, that all was not well, they were not sufficient to cause great alarm to the rank and file of supporters. They continued to read the monthly magazine, and those who attended the 1913 Conference Hall meetings were probably no more aware of impending disaster than were the distinguished, wealthy passengers aboard the mighty Titanic as it steamed on its maiden voyage across the Atlantic. If those passengers had even noticed the tips of icebergs in the calm waters, the sight would not have disturbed them. The Titanic was known to be unsinkable! Even when a shudder went through the great liner, followed by the shutting off of the engines, they continued with their dignified merry-making until the incredible announcement that the lifeboats were being manned, accompanied by the undoubted list of the vessel, convinced them that it was going down fast. Within a matter of hours it was at the bottom of the ocean, with only a few survivors in the inadequate supply of lifeboats that bobbed up and down on the smooth, icy-cold waters.

The news flashed round the world like an evil portent. It

was strangely disturbing. What next?

In August, 1914, the Prussian armies marched across the Belgian frontier and Great Britain declared war on Germany. That year the annual report of the Mildmay institutions and missions came out as usual, and contained an entertaining little report by Miss M. A. Bellamy, the hospital Deputation Secretary, of how the war had unfortunately prevented her visiting Britanny, as planned, so she had gone somewhere else instead. When she wrote it she no doubt thought, like nearly everyone else, that it would all be over by Christmas.

But it was not all over by Christmas. It dragged on for four sad, weary years. The khaki-clad young men stepping it out smartly to 'Rule Britannia' and 'Land of Hope and Glory' knew very well when they marched down to the sea to board the Channel boats that they would probably never march back again. Nearly two million of them never did. As for the annual report of the Mildmay institutions and missions, the one produced for 1914 was the last of its kind. Were they, like the Titanic, to quietly sink out of sight?

Chapter Four

SURVIVAL

Bessie sat looking with dismay out of the carriage window at the dreary rows of tenement buildings, concrete courts and narrow alleys that slid slowly by as the train drew towards Paddington. Washing was hanging out of windows, flapping limply like decaying vegetation in a slimy gorge, and a dreary haze enfolded everything. She was drawing near to the end of her first train journey, and asked herself in alarm what she was coming to. It was all so different from her native Gloucestershire, with its woods and its fields and its clean, self-respecting little villages nestling on the hills. And when she was eventually deposited with her tin trunk at the Mildmay Mission Hospital in Bethnal Green, the place overawed her. It looked so drab and battered, the hissing gas-light casting sinister shadows along the stone corridors and shabby rooms, and everything needing a fresh coat of paint. Bessie, alone in the tiny room with the big bed which she was to share with another domestic, was overcome by the strangeness of it all. Her blue eyes filled with tears, her rosy-cheeked little face crumpled up, and she longed for home.

It was 1918, and the Great War had been dragging on for four years, the young manhood of the nation in the forefront, 'fodder for the guns'. Those who were shattered and maimed, but still had life in them, were shipped back to England, manfully trying to sing,

'Take me back to dear old Blighty,
Put me on the train for London Town . . .'

The nurses who worked at the base camps never knew what they might be confronted with as the hospital trains drew into the great terminii, and were slowly relieved of their human cargo. Grace Josephine Wakefield Bragg did not know whether to laugh or cry that day when she saw with amazement that her own husband was on one of the stretchers. They had come back from China on their first leave, and the outbreak of war had prevented them returning. Tom, of course, had been called up and sent to the front, and now here he was, invalided, but thank God alive, and most miraculously brought to the very place where she was working.

It turned out very well for the Mildmay Mission Hospital, too, that Dr Tom Bragg had got a 'Blighty' wound. The little hospital in the East End was putting up a fight for its own existence just about that time, battling against a variety of odds, one of which was a shortage of doctors. They had nearly all gone to the war, and the need had become so acute at Mildmay that old Dr Gauld had come out of retirement to take a clinic a couple of days a week. Now here was Dr Tom Bragg free for a few months, and glad to fill a gap. In such ways Mildmay managed to keep its head above water medically, with the doctors and nurses working until they nearly dropped.

But there was more to running the hospital than depended on the medical staff. Those who were responsible for ways and means were up against it, too. They listened to the treasurer's reports, and prayed earnestly that God would meet their needs, at the same time applying their minds to the problem of how economies could be practised and funds raised.

'God and my right hand' might not have been their conscious motto, but it was the principle on which they worked. If the well-dressed ladies in their smart tailor-mades, and the gentlemen in their frock coats and highly polished boots appeared but seldom in the hospital itself, the hospital appeared frequently in their conversation and correspondence, as well as in their prayers. They organised sales of work, held garden parties and drawing-room meetings, they sent baskets of fruit and vegetables, and enlisted the patronage of influential people. The collecting of old bottles for medicines, and the cutting up of old sheets for bandages was not beneath them, and they were always on the alert for equipment that might be obtained at reduced prices.

Not for merely casual reading did they peruse *The Times*. They kept their eyes as well as their ears open for anything that might affect the hospital. The passing of the National Insurance Act filled them with apprehension, and they wondered what it might lead to. They concurred wholeheartedly with those who were protesting against the low salaries paid to members of the nursing profession, and 'felt confident that subscribers would approve of their action in ensuring that nurses and sisters at Mildmay were paid an adequate living wage'.

The subscribers and donors had to be kept in touch with what was going on, that their interest and support might be maintained. Had it not been for Miss Bellamy's energetic and enterprising deputation work, her encouragement to the 'King's Daughters' and the 'Royal Service', the 'Brotherhood Box Holders Association' and the 'Busy Bee Band' in their respective efforts to contribute to the upkeep, one wonders how the hospital would have survived at all. This gay and imaginative person was especially successful with children, and the Busy Bees, of which she was the Queen Bee, were constantly regaled with the conversations which took place between the plane tree in the hospital courtyard and the little bird who reported all that was going on in the wards.

But times were hard and taxation was getting heavier. The wealthy supporters who had borne most of the financial burden of the hospital were nearly all gone, and legacies were running out. Enough money had been raised for an electrically controlled lift and the installation of electric light in the operating theatre, but the rest of the hospital would have to wait. The renewal of the whole drainage system had become an urgent priority. When it came to a choice between sewers and electric lights, sewers won the day. There wasn't enough money for both, with an average expenditure of £5,000 and a fixed income of only £320 drawn from investments.

Shortage of money was not the worst of it, however. There was something else that weighed heavily on the minds and hearts of those whose task it was to keep the wheels turning. The great Mildmay organisation itself, of which the Mission Hospital was only one of many branches, was in a process of disintegration. The old order was changing, and a different spirit seemed to have crept in. One lady who had raised a lot of money for one of the Mildmay institutions had then demanded to take it over altogether. That was not the only problem, either. After many committee meetings and solicitors' letters, consultations and prayer meetings, things came to a head, and it was decided that each of the Mildmay institutions must henceforth look after its own affairs and be self-supporting. The Mildmay Mission Hospital at Bethnal Green, the Medical Mission at Old Ford, the Convalescent Home, the Bible Flower Mission, the Mission to the Jews and all the rest, must make their own way now. Sink or swim!

Some sank and some swam. In retrospect it is easy to see that out of the disintegration good came. Organisations whose usefulness belonged to a former generation were wound up, and those that were in danger of being hampered by tradition and mismanagement were freed.

In 1918 it was not so easy to see the advantages however. So what with all this inner turmoil that had to be kept as secret as possible, and what with the War still dragging on months after Allenby had marched triumphantly into Jerusalem to make sense of the Balfour Declaration* it is not surprising that the Mildmay Mission Hospital looked very much the worse for wear, and nearly at its last gasp, and that Bessie was almost submerged with homesickness in her first few days there.

If it had not been for Sister Frances Arbuthnot, Bessie would never have left the village in Gloucestershire to come to Mildmay at all. Sister Arbuthnot was the Squire's niece, and all the villagers agreed that she was an angel. She came to stay with her uncle and aunt from time to time, and when she did so she talked about the Hospital near Shoreditch church, and how she loved being there, and what a great privilege it was to work for God. So when she asked Bessie, who had not long left school, if she would come up to London to work in the hospital as a maid, Bessie said, yes, she would. It would be wonderful to be working in the same place as Miss Arbuthnot, she thought.

Bessie had been brought up to be clean and tidy and work hard, tell the truth and keep the law. If Miss Arbuthnot shrewdly guessed that there was still some-

* The Balfour Declaration announced that 'His Majesty's Government views with favour the establishment in Palestine of a national home for the Jewish people, and will use their best endeavours to facilitate this object'.

thing lacking, she did not say so, and Bessie arrived at Mildmay, like many another, a little apprehensive as to whether or not she could do the work satisfactorily, but with no question as to whether she was all a Christian ought to be. It was not until she noticed the way Fanny said her prayers that she began to have her doubts.

Fanny was the fellow domestic with whom she shared the bedroom. Fanny was even smaller than Bessie, Jewish by race, but she was a Christian and said so, which Bessie thought rather surprising. She had lost both her parents, and been brought up in an orphanage, and you wouldn't have thought she had much to be happy about, but she was happy. She said her prayers as though she liked doing it, staying on her knees for what seemed to Bessie a very long time, and eventually rising with a contented expression on her little face, as though she had just returned from some very happy and satisfying encounter. She talked about the Lord Jesus, too, as though she knew Him, and loved Him.

This was all faintly disturbing, since Bessie did not feel that way at all, but she had not been in Mildmay long before she realised that the nurses and the sisters felt just the same as Fanny. She heard them talking about 'the Lord', His wonderful kindness, the way He had answered their prayers, and whether or not a certain course of action would please Him. They did it not only in the religious meetings, when it might have been expected, but in every-day conversation. And although they were, after all, ordinary human beings like herself, prone to irritation when tired, to day-dreaming too, and even to failure in duty, there was a kindliness and sincerity about them which warmed Bessie's heart and quite dispelled the home-sickness.

'They were all sweet,' she said many years later, 'you couldn't help loving them.' Though she admitted, 'But some of them had got that little extra something that made you love them just that little bit more.'

Not but what she was always completely respectful, of course, for Bessie accepted her position as a serving maid without the slightest resentment. 'You knew they were your betters, but even if they scolded you, you knew it was for your good. There was a love between us all – it was like one big family. And Matron – she was strict, but you knew she was just.'

In the end, it was through Matron that Bessie got to the place where she knew 'the Lord', just as the others knew Him. Matron was leading a Sunday evening meeting in the Mission Hall, and she took the fifty-third chapter of the book of Isaiah as the basis of her talk.

'All we like sheep have gone astray; we have turned every one to his own way; and the Lord hath laid on Him the iniquity of us all. . . . '

Perhaps Bessie had heard little lambs who had wandered away bleating piteously among the briars until the hands of the shepherd, ruthlessly indifferent to the thorns but very gentle with the trembling little creatures, lifted them to a place of safety. Perhaps some flash of insight told her that she was not unlike a foolish little lamb herself, liable to wander off into horrible entanglements from which she could not extricate herself. Perhaps some deeper revelation showed her the hands of the Shepherd, ruthlessly enduring the piercing of nails in order to deliver her from the way that led to death and set her on the way to Life.

Whatever it was Miss Dora Woodhouse said that Sunday evening Bessie could not quite remember. All she knew was that she fled from the Hall in tears, stumbled up to her bedroom, and lay on the bed, Fanny beside her, both of them crying softly, with gentle little sobs bubbling up from the depths of their beings. Fanny was crying for joy because God had answered her prayers for her friend, and Bessie because her heart seemed so melted with love that she couldn't do anything else. A new world seemed to be opening up to her, invisible to the naked eye, but intensely real to her awakened spirit, a world governed by the Lord Who planned everything for the good of His people. The very next morning she went to find Sister Arbuthnot, and told her with shining eyes that Jesus had come into her life, and she knew now what it meant to be born again.

It was about a couple of years later that Percy appeared on the scene. He was Mr Bower's youngest son, slim and dark and wiry, and a great help he was to Mum, pushing her barrow up to the market on Kingsland Road where she had a stall for second-hand clothes and things. He did a lot of pushing of barrows, did Percy, piled high with wardrobes from the workshops of the Jewish cabinet makers who had settled in the East End. These Jewish refugees from the pogroms in Russia had flowed like a new current from the London docks to Golders Green, their business acumen and hard work bringing welcome employment in their train. Percy observed that a Jew would sell something for a halfpenny more than he had paid for it and be satisfied where other people expected twopence profit and often enough failed to effect a sale! Small profits, quick returns was their motto. If he was not so astute at business as the Jewish employers, at any rate Percy had an equal capacity for hard work when he was able to get it, and when there was the need for another porter at the Mildmay, Percy got the job.

His duties included working the hand lift on which food was sent up to the wards from the kitchen, and it so happened that Bessie's duties included taking the food from the lift and conveying it to Tankerville Ward, where she worked. Doctors walked along the corridor, nurses and sisters hurried by, but none of them noticed when a little bar of chocolate was put on the lift that went speeding up to Tankerville Ward, Percy heaving away at the rope. And when the lift came to a standstill nobody saw that Bessie, with a little blush and a quick look round, slipped the chocolate into her pocket before she trotted briskly away, pushing the trolley with the patients' food.

The time came when Percy asked if he could take her for a walk on her evening out, and together they walked along the streets of Bethnal Green, rather self-consciously since it was the first time it had happened. There was something Percy very much wanted to know about Bessie.

'Are you a Christian?' he asked her outright.

'Yes, I am,' replied Bessie firmly. She told him all about that Sunday night when Matron had spoken on the fifty-third chapter of Isaiah, and how she had realised then that Jesus had died on the cross for her, and how life had been quite different for her since then.

He'd never had an experience like that, Percy told her, but he felt just like she did, and believed that when Jesus died on the cross He bore the sins of Percy Bower, along with those of all the world. He'd seen a miracle happen in his own family, too, when his eldest sister's husband had been changed into a different man overnight. A fierce bare-fist fighter was his brother-in-law, famous in the boxing rings of the East End for the way he could knock 'em out. But one night he'd found himself in a tight corner, threatened by a gang out to give him the worst beating up of his life, and in his distress he had prayed urgently, 'Oh, God, get me out of this, and I'll serve you for ever!' God had got him out, and that experience had revolutionised him. He had made a vow to the God who is alive, and by God's grace he'd kept it! There used to be awful rows at home before it happened – so bad that Mum and Percy and Ernest used to get out and walk the streets till things quietened down. But it was all different now, and the change in his brother-in-law was amazing. No fights at home now! Percy could safely take Bessie along to meet Mum, which he did. It was the right and proper thing to do, now they were walking out.

The same year that Percy was taken on as a porter, Dr White, a missionary from Persia, was appointed medical superintendent. Dr White had quite a way with him, listening courteously to his patients, and prescribing with due regard to their suggestions.

'Dr Vite! That vite medicine you gave me is no good. Please change it!'

Certainly! He had a quiet word with the dispenser about adding a little colour and the lady went triumphantly off with a bottle of ruby red mixture which did her the world of good. He never showed the least surprise when Miss Rosie came along to the surgery on Friday, looking remarkably like Mrs Rosenberg who had been in on Tuesday, and bearing a striking resemblance to Mrs Rosestein who had attended last week. Whether it was three ladies once or one lady three times made no difference to Dr White, apart from the little twinkle that came in his eye as he solemnly wrote his record on the appropriate card.

It was during his eighteen years in office that the State Registration of Nurses was introduced, and Mildmay obtained recognition as a Nurses Training School. It was gratifying to know that it was up to standard – in spite of the poor condition of the nurses' home. The Medical Committee in 1914 had passed a resolution that increased accommodation for nurses was urgently necessary. That was ten years ago, and the only change in the situation was that it was now even more urgently necessary. What with the trade depression and the general unrest of the 1920's, the Council was hard put to it to spread an income of about £10,000 over the running costs of a voluntary hospital treating some 50,000 out-patients and 1,200 in-patients annually, without attempting to do anything in the way of building extensions.

But now something must be done, the Council decided, and something was done. Those little prayer meetings that were a feature of the place began to combine practical requests for the money required for a new nurses' home in the same breath as ardent strivings for deepened love, increased humility, and the conversion of men and women to repentance and faith in Christ. And in various ways, largely unexpected, from donations and legacies and the tapping of resources in organisations dedicated to assisting good causes, the money came in. The balance sheets showed entries running into many hundreds of pounds, along with those running into hundreds of pence gained by the sale of postcards, and silver paper. There was no waste in the Mildmay Mission Hospital, and if old iron and junk could be turned into cash, turned into cash it was.

In 1926, in spite of the General Strike, the foundation stone of the new extension was well and truly laid by the Lord Mayor of London, to whom the vote of thanks was delivered by Sir George Hume, Chairman of the London County Council. The young nurses who watched the ceremony looked down modestly as it was asserted that they who had so much hard work and anxiety, and so much overtime, ought to have comfortable quarters in which to live. They kept their exuberance in until they could give vent to it in private. At last the long-hoped-for single bedroom apiece was on the way to becoming a reality!

When Nurse Maude from Essex started her training, however, there was no such luxurious privacy. She had to share a room like all the others, and of course could only go to see her parents once a week. There was too much to be done in the hospital even when the nurses were not on duty in the wards to allow much time off. The making of pillow cases and mending of sheets, washing out of bottles and counting of laundry was part of the day's work, as well as the addressing of envelopes and the sending out of the magazine.

Maude took it all cheerfully, and tried to be very careful when handling equipment, for as Sister Arbuthnot reminded her.

'You won't be able to run round the corner and buy what you want when you're on the mission field, you know. Better learn to look after things now.'

Maude had come to Mildmay because she wanted to be a missionary as well as a nurse, and the Mission Hospital in London's East End seemed the best place to get training for this dual purpose. She wasn't afraid of hard work, she liked people and so enjoyed looking after the patients. She had plenty of common sense, too, and realising that she had a lot to learn, accepted correction and sometimes a scolding with the minimum of depression or resentment.

There was one thing, however, that she really could not stand, and that was drunkenness. Her parents were Baptists and firm teetotallers, and she hated the very smell of beer. The sight of men lurching about all the worse for drink was what she disliked most about Bethnal Green, and it made her hurry all the quicker to get away from the streets and into the clean, shady courtyard of the Mildmay.

So when, in her second year, she was on night duty, and was called down to the Casualty Department to help with a drunken man who had been brought in, pouring with blood, from a brawl, she went down the stairs from her well-conducted ward apprehensively. The sight that met her eyes did nothing to reassure her, for the man's face was so battered and bleeding that she could not see whether he was young or old, and he was struggling so violently that the nurse and the doctor could not hold him down.

'Call Percy!' they gasped. 'Percy! Percy!' Percy came bounding up from his bedroom in the basement at the double, and between them all they managed to get the man on the operating table. The only way to keep him there was to hold him down, so Percy sat on him while the doctor gave him a whiff of chloroform. Then the team got to work, everyone doing his job as efficiently as a well-oiled machine.

The Night Sister turned to Nurse Maude.

'Go up and get a bed ready for him,' she said.

Maude gasped. The man was struggling and swearing at the top of his voice.

'Oh! Have I got to have him in my ward?' she asked.

'Of course!' The Sister looked at her with faint surprise. There was only one man's ward in the hospital. 'Where else?'

Maude went back up the stairs, nearly sick with fright, to make the bed ready.

Chapter Five

VOLUNTARY HOSPITALS IN THE RED

When Charlie Haynes was brought into the Mildmay Mission Hospital that night in the 1920's, the police already knew a lot about him. He was one of eight children of a drunken father, living in an alley that backed on the mortuary. He'd been sent to Sunday School, like most of the other kids in the neighbourhood, but as soon as he got into long trousers he decided he was too big for all that sort of thing, and went roaming the streets with the boys, making a nuisance of himself and getting into trouble with the police. They warned him he'd get to Borstal if he didn't change his ways. He had joined the Grenadier Guards, but in after years admitted that he only spent 43 days with the regiment – the rest of his two years in the Guards he was in detention. He'd made an effort to reform once or twice, but nothing came of it, and now there were one or two safe-breaking incidents the police might have asked him about if only they had had sufficient evidence. A couple of them were ready to question him about the brawl when he eventually came to his senses in Mathieson ward, after a night when he'd been swearing so profanely that even his father, who had been called to his bedside, muttered warningly,

'You mustn't say things like that in here!'

Charlie Haynes was a notorious character, and news of what had happened got all round the hospital in a very short time. 'Young Charlie Haynes brought in drunk as a lord last night, been involved in an awful fight, police questioning him by his bedside right now!'

His name was on everybody's lips. One of the worst characters in the neighbourhood had been brought right into their midst. What a challenge! What an opportunity! At prayer meetings, public and private, he was a main topic for intercession. Down in the basement the Cockney voices of Percy and Ernest Bower were raised in earnest prayer that God would have mercy on Charlie Haynes, in the nurses' sitting room girlish voices pleaded that he might repent and be saved, when the doctors and the matron had a few minutes together to pray over hospital affairs, the name of Charlie Haynes found its way in.

Any little bit of news about his progress was eagerly passed on. He was a very likeable young fellow when sober, it was reported, willing to lend a hand at moving heavy screens, and heavy patients too, all with a cheerful grin. When it came to ward services, however, he made it plain they were not in his line. And he couldn't stand the texts on the walls.

'When can I get out of this?' he asked repeatedly. It wasn't very encouraging, but the voices kept on praying...

Nurse Maude was on duty on the day when Charlie was discharged, and she had to lead the ward service. Leading the ward service for people like Charlie, who didn't want to listen, was rather an ordeal, and she felt quite nervous, especially when it came to praying aloud. But she was not one to shirk her duty, nor to evade reality, and since Charlie was leaving the ward that day, she included him in her prayer.

'Bless the one who is going out today,' she prayed. 'May he realise that he need not go out alone. May he realise that Thou art with him,' she went on, and there was a little break in her voice, 'Reveal Thyself to him, Lord.'

An hour or two later she was giving out medicines to the patients, and could not see Charlie, so went in search of him. She found him in the bathroom.

'Here, Charlie, your medicine!' she said. Then she looked at his face, and her tone changed.

'Are you all right?' she asked with concern. He looked as though he had been crying.

'I'm all right,' he mumbled. He's sorry to be leaving, she thought. Patients were often sorry to leave the pleasant security and orderliness of the hospital to go back to their own uncertain and disturbing lives.

'Cheer up,' she said. 'You'll feel fine once you're out and about again . . . ' Before he left she gave him a little New Testament.

'I hope you'll read it,' she said. Then she added, rather surprisingly in view of his avowed distaste for religion, 'If you want to know more about things you can come back to the ward at visiting times, for the ward service you know. And we hope you'll come along to the meetings in the Mission Hall.' Then she said goodbye, and left him.

Within a day or two the rumour was going round the hospital that Charlie Haynes was converted. Percy was sure of it – had taken him home to Mum for a cup of cocoa and a chat, and Charlie was quite changed. The day he'd come out of hospital he'd gone back to his family and told them he was a Christian now. Standing in the kitchen, with the old sink and the pots and the pans and the wet washing hanging on a line slung across the room, he had warned them that if they didn't repent and believe in Christ, they'd all go to hell. What he lacked in tact he made up for in sincerity.

One day Nurse Maude, walking briskly along the cobbled Austin Street, saw a group of people at the corner, and heard the familiar sound of open-air preaching. Then she realised that the voice was familiar, too. With a start of surprise she saw Charlie, standing on a box, and thumbing in the direction of the public house.

'I've spent hours in there,' he was saying as she passed. 'Spent hours in there, I have, and lots of money, too, but I'm finished with all that now. The Lord has saved me, and He's changed my life. . . . '

Maude passed on, marvelling, but the crowd remained to listen, and talk about what had happened to Charlie. It was, in fact, the talk of the neighbourhood for many a day. Some said that Charlie turned teetotaller wouldn't last, that he'd had a fright but would get over it, and the sooner the better. Others stoutly affirmed that he was a changed man and all the better for it, and it was to be hoped that others would follow his example. Charlie was providing a talking point for all who enjoyed talking.

Some time later one of the doctors in the hospital went in search of Maude.

'I met Charlie Haynes just now,' the doctor said, 'And he asked me to give you a message. He wants you to know that the others involved in the fight have all been let off, too, and he's very glad about it. "As a Christian, I know I was at fault as well as them," he said. He wanted me to tell you.'

Maude was faintly surprised that the message should have been sent to her. Why single her out? But then, she thought, he knew that she was interested in him, since he had been converted in the ward where she was working. Wishing to encourage him still further in the Christian way of life, she invited him to attend a special meeting being planned in her church at home. 'Can I bring him back here to tea first?' she asked her parents. 'You'll be interested to meet him – you've heard so much about him. Now you can see for yourselves what he's like.'

Her parents were not as prompt to agree as she had expected. They were not snobs, too proud to have a young fellow from the slums in their home for a meal. She knew they were not like that, so why did they hesitate? She was even more surprised when, giving a rather grudging consent, her father said,

'I hope this doesn't lead to anything.'

'Lead to anything!' Whatever did father mean? 'He's just a young convert we want to help!'

But it did lead to something – something of a very disturbing nature. For one day she walked with Charlie to the bus stop after a meeting, and just before he swung himself up onto the bus he bent down and kissed her.

Maude was horrified. She couldn't allow that! She turned away and hurried off, alarmed at the thought that someone who knew her might have seen what happened. And whatever was Charlie thinking of! She must do something about this. It must never be allowed to happen again.

The question was, what should she do? Two or three days passed, and before she could make up her mind what to do and how to do it, the thing happened again – and this time right in the hospital itself.

She was walking along the corridor that led to the Mission Hall in the course of her duties when she noticed that someone was sitting on the window sill. It was Charlie. The men's meeting was due to commence in about half-an-hour's time, and there he was, waiting for it. There was no keeping him from the meetings now. His zeal was unabated, as those who had prophesied an early declension had to admit. Charlie had become a regular Bible thumper! No one else was in the corridor, and Maude had to pass right by him. There was no way of escape, and before she knew what he was doing he had slipped down, bent over her, and gently kissed her cheek.

She remained outwardly calm, hurrying on without a word, but her mind was in a turmoil. Whatever would happen if Matron got to know that one of her nurses had been kissed in the corridor! And what did Charlie mean by it? Strangely enough, she found she could not be at all angry with him, though she refused to yield to the insidious suggestion that what he had done was really rather nice. It was wrong, definitely wrong, and she must put a stop to it.

She therefore wrote him a little letter, saying that she did not know what he was thinking about her, but as far as she was concerned, she knew what she thought about him. He was a friend, nothing more. She didn't exactly say that as such he should be careful not to take liberties, but she tried to imply it, kindly but firmly.

That letter was all Charlie needed, for he was longing to tell her what he was thinking about her. When he first saw her bending over him up in Mathieson ward as he was slowly coming round, his head swathed in bandages, he thought she was an angel, with her halo-like cap, and her kindly, impersonal eyes. He did not tell her with what interest he became aware that she was, like himself, in the flesh and blood category instead, nor did he mention that he found the slow twinkle that came sometimes into her eyes, seeming to well up from some deep source of benevolent wisdom, infinitely intriguing. What he did say was that there was something he wanted to have a talk to her about, and would she meet him somewhere?

Maude agreed to meet him. This would give her the opportunity to tell him that when she had finished her nursing training she planned to join the Regions Beyond Missionary Union, and go overseas as a missionary. That, she felt, would make the position plain, and put a stop to Charlie's thinking of anything that might, as her father would have expressed it, lead to something. She was rather taken aback, therefore, when he said,

'I feel God is calling me into full time service, too.'

'Oh!'

'And I believe it is God who has brought us together . . . ' he went on.

It was quite a long time before Maude allowed herself to consider this possibility seriously. However, eventually she was forced to the conclusion that this new Charlie had a faith and a conviction that seemed sometimes to surpass her own. All right, she was willing to marry him if that were God's will – but God's will, and God's service, must come first. If God made it plain that He was calling Charlie into His service, then she, Maude, would be prepared to believe He was leading them to serve Him together.

Then Charlie, in a very unexpected way, went off for two years to get Bible training. It was something he had longed for, and without which he would be unequipped for missionary work anywhere – but he had no money to pay college fees, no well-to-do relatives or friends to help him, so how could he obtain it? Charlie did not know, and all he could do was to ask his Heavenly Master to provide what he needed – and his Heavenly Master did so.

This is how it came about. One of the Mildmay Mission Hospital sisters heard of his desire, and felt constrained to offer to pay for him to go through a Bible College. He could go to whichever one he chose, she told him. Charlie knew nothing about any of them, but a friend suggested the Glasgow Bible Training Institute would be the place for him. So off he went. From various unpredictable sources other practical needs were met, in the way these things happen to people who launch out in the confidence that God is alive, and has called them to do a job for him. Maude came right round to believing that Charlie was right, and it was God's plan for them to serve him together. It would be on the foreign mission field, of course, since that was where God meant to send her.

Then something happened which brought her to a standstill and confronted her with the fact that she had been wrong about God's will, after all. What happened had nothing whatever to do with Charlie – it had to do with her. She had a serious haemorrhage. This, followed by an adverse medical report, resulted in the door closing to her to go abroad as a Regions Beyond missionary. Maude, with tight determined lips, wrote to tell Charlie of the irrevocable decision, and said that on no account would she stand in his way. He must go forward without her.

Charlie agreed to pray about it, and not to correspond with her until he knew what he ought to do, but after a week of silence she heard from him again. It all came back to what he had told her right at the start – he believed God was calling him to full-time service, and that God meant them to serve Him together till death should them part. . . .

So that story had a happy ending, not with Charlie going to the foreign mission field as Maude's husband, but with Maude remaining in England as the wife of Charlie Haynes, who joined the London City Mission; a subtle distinction which brought the whole relationship into line. And that, incidentally, is how Miss Dora Woodhouse, Matron of the Mildmay, lost another of her good nurses.

Miss Dora Woodhouse was always losing her good nurses, it seemed. Either they got married, or went abroad as missionaries, or both. She herself had steered a course clear of either, for she was first and last a Mildmay Deaconess. She had gone into training in the Deaconess Home in her early twenties, and while there had been sent to help in the Mildmay Mission Hospital's out-patients department for three days a week for three months. During those three months she found her true vocation as a nurse, entered the hospital as a probationer, paying her fee of thirteen guineas and providing her own uniform, of course. The financial side of things presented no difficulty. Her father, who was a vicar, could afford to support his daughter. That was away back in 1910, and now, in the 1920's, she was the Matron, a queen in her own right, gracious and dignified, with the sort of clear blue eyes that seemed to look right through you. She could be a disconcerting person to encounter, as more than one nursing applicant discovered at the first interview.

'And when were you converted?' she would ask. It was all right if you knew what she meant, and had had the experience yourself, but if, like Ethel Noakes, you thought she meant, 'When were you confirmed?' and told her the date, and then discovered she didn't mean that at all, it was embarrassing to say the least of it.

Ethel was more than embarrassed – she was downright angry, although she managed to keep it in until afterwards. At the age of nineteen she was full of good intentions and high ideals, planning to be a missionary, having heard David Livingstone preach in the village where she lived. One day, turning over the pages of a telephone directory, she saw the words, 'Mildmay Mission Hospital, Bethnal Green', and decided at once that this was the place for her. Bethnal Green was in the East End, she knew, right in the slums where, as her mother had told her, the people were in rags, went about without shoes, and were very, very poor. The hospital was a Mission hospital, so where better to start her career? With a sense of her own nobility at being prepared for a life of hardship and self-sacrifice she made her application, only to find that in some inexplicable way she came short of what was required. For after giving the date of her confirmation, and trying to answer a few questions of an obtrusive nature which she really could not understand, that dignified blue-eyed Matron had exclaimed,

'But, my dear – you're not converted!'

Converted! Ethel had heard the word, and connected it with the Salvation Army and the Plymouth Brethren, the sort of people who held open-air meetings on street corners. 'I suppose she's one of them,' thought Maude, rather surprised that one with such dignity should have such low associations. She was still more surprised when, in the course of the short conversation, Matron let out that she was the daughter of a Church of England clergyman. The outcome of the interview was that Ethel's application was politely rejected, and she walked away from the Hospital with indignation boiling in her heart, and a little booklet called *Safety, Certainty and Enjoyment* crammed indifferently into her handbag.

Six months later Matron had another letter from Ethel Noakes, saying she now knew what Matron meant by being converted, since it had happened to her. Again she was applying for nursing training in the Mildmay Mission Hospital, and this time when Matron interviewed her it was quite another story. Although she was too young to enter as a probationer (no one under 21 was eligible at that time), Matron would take her on as a house helper until she was old enough to start her training. So in went Ethel, and a very satisfactory nurse she became, especially in the children's ward, where she was in her element at Christmas time, decorating the tree, blowing up balloons, preparing exciting parcels for all the children and filling their pillow cases with toys.

'Nurse, what is this?' asked a little Jewish boy in wonderment.

'Oh, it's because it's Christmas day,' she replied, beaming at him. 'All these toys in this pillow case are for you.'

'But why?' asked the lad.

'It's Jesus' birthday, so it's a specially happy day for us all. He came as a baby many years ago,' she continued. 'He came as a baby, and He came into this world to be our Saviour. . . . He loves us, and wants us to be happy.'

The dark-eyed little Jew lapsed into silence, looking almost absent-mindedly at all his parcels. Then he looked up at her, and said rather quietly,

'I wish we had a Jesus in our religion.'

Nurse Noakes never forgot that incident, and she had a way of relating it that made it difficult for others to forget it, either, as with eyes aglow she went on, 'What a wonderful thing to be able to tell him that Jesus *is* in his religion!' For Nurse Noakes, like all the other Mildmay nurses, had to be ready to take her turn at ward services, and in addition to becoming a good nurse became a good speaker into the bargain. But she, too, moved out of Mildmay towards the mission field, and, as it happened, matrimony as well. . . . Miss Woodhouse was always losing her good nurses!

It is doubtful whether the loss of a good nurse caused the matron of Mildmay nearly so much anxiety as the threatened loss of Percy the porter, though. Percy was married to Bessie by this time, living in one room in Mum's house. The brass knobs on the fender gleamed and sparkled from Percy's diligent rubbing, and Bessie saw to it that the curtains at the windows were always crisp and clean, no matter how thick the fogs were that crawled and crept into every nook and cranny of the East End in those days. That room was home, the place of warmth and comfort and love, from which they set out together on a Sunday spruce and speckless in their well-brushed Salvation

Army uniforms, and to which they returned to look round with pride at the photographs and ornaments on the mantelpiece, the pictures and texts on the wall, the spotless bed cover and the polished lino.

When a baby arrived, and then another, and then another, they had to readjust their programme. Bessie couldn't get to the meetings as easily as before, though she usually managed to get to those at Mildmay. It was understood that Percy must keep up his open-air preaching, and teaching in Sunday School, and going to the Citadel at Clapton at least once on Sunday. Bessie, pushing the pram along to meet him, toddlers and all, waved happily when he came in sight, while he quickened his steps, smiling to see his little family like an overloaded boat, swaying towards him along the pavement.

It was the fast increasing appetite of the fast increasing little family, and the eldest one growing out of her clothes so quickly there was always something needing to be bought, that brought an anxious pucker on Bessie's forehead as she told Percy about it, and made him frown as he counted over his money and saw that after the rent had been paid, and due allowance made for the week's housekeeping, it would be a month before they could get enough saved up for a new pair of shoes.

'It's a job making ends meet,' they agreed, and although Bessie knew at just which stalls in the market she could get things cheaper by half a penny a pound than anywhere else, and although Percy was always on the look-out for an odd job of carpentering or cobbling that would bring in a little extra money, the time came when Percy said heavily that he wondered if he'd better get another job, for the kids' sakes. He'd learned how to do french polishing, and men working on that could earn a tidy bit, more than he'd ever get as a porter. There was a vacancy coming up soon, he'd heard . . . He thought he'd better give in his notice at Mildmay.

Bessie sighed. She knew what it would mean to him to leave the place – what it would mean to her, too, for that matter. They'd still go along to the meetings, of course, but it wouldn't be the same. They wouldn't *belong* any more. Maybe Percy would still be invited to speak at the men's meeting sometimes, but there would be someone else on the door, someone else keeping an eye on things. Percy would just have to sit as one of the congregation – no responsibility, like. And he'd be wondering how things were going on down in the basement, whether the drains were being kept clean, whether the back doors and windows were properly locked and bolted at night. And if there was an emergency, as there so often was, they wouldn't be able to call him. He wouldn't be there.

If it weren't for the children they wouldn't even consider it, Percy and Bessie agreed. They'd make do gladly, like they always had done. Better be at the Mildmay on a low wage than anywhere else on a high one. But it was the children. . . .

So Percy told Miss Woodhouse. He was sorry, more sorry than he could say, but he'd have to leave. It wasn't that he was dissatisfied, or didn't like the work, or anything like that. He loved the place. He was leaving only for one reason. He and Bessie couldn't make ends meet, now that there were four little ones to feed and clothe. He'd have to earn more money to keep them.

Miss Woodhouse listened quietly. Yes, she understood his difficulty. She did not need to say much, or to remind him that most of those working at the Mildmay were doing it for a lower salary than they could get elsewhere. Percy knew that as well as she did, and that voluntary hospitals were usually in the red. It was becoming more and more difficult to run them efficiently, with donations dropping as taxation came increasingly heavily on the sort of people who in the past had been the chief supporters. It was the large number of small subscriptions rather than the small number of large ones that was keeping the Mildmay going now. All she could do after she had listened to what Percy had to say, was to suggest that they should pray about it together, which they did, standing with heads bowed in Matron's dark little sitting room with its window facing the brick wall of the new lift shaft. Then she asked him to think about the matter and pray about it a little longer before making up his mind.

So Percy did as she asked, and talked it over with Miss Hancock as well. Miss Hancock knew Percy better than anyone else in the hospital, where she was a sort of unofficial mother to many. She was the Lady Almoner, and to her was entrusted the task of finding out the really needy people, and quietly disbursing practical aid from a little store of money and provisions allocated for that purpose, as well as helping them to fill in forms and make applications to august bodies who existed to defend their rights, but about whom most of them had never heard. She had the qualities required for this sort of job, a warm heart and a level head, and an intense interest in human beings. Added to these was an indefinable quality, a sort of self-giving which encouraged people to confide in her. Percy had known her from the time he was a lad, coming to the Gospel meetings she so often led, and many had been the occasion when, looking straight into her friendly eyes, he had told her his experiences, and she had responded by sharing some of hers. All sense of natural gulfs of age and social position dissolved in those brief, deep talks, when she told him how once she had loved a man, a Jew, and he had loved her. But the Jew would not admit Jesus into his religion, and Miss Hancock could not keep Jesus out of hers,

'So, of course, I could go no further.' It had obviously cost so much, that renunciation, that Percy sensed the confidence she had in him for her even to tell him of it. It was easy, therefore, to confide his own financial difficulty, for she would know he was not doing so to try and get extra help. No thought of that even entered Percy's head, nor hers either. The Lady Almoner had no favourites when it came to disbursing charity. Prayer was another matter, and she really couldn't help it if he came in for a specially large place in her intercessions.

'Let us pray about it,' she said when he told her he thought he would have to get another job. And after she had prayed, asking God to show Percy where *He* wanted him, asking God to provide for his needs and to strengthen him, Percy went home to talk it all over again with Bessie. Between them they went over the budget yet again, and Bessie thought of one or two more economies she could work out, and Percy reckoned that if he could pick up a few more odd jobs in his spare time, window-cleaning and the like, they could manage. Behind all the contriving and the scheming and the keeping on the lookout for bargains and odd jobs, there was that deep love for the Mildmay, and the conviction, hard to put into words, that God had appointed Percy to be a porter there.

'And I wouldn't want to be anywhere else,' said Percy, and told Matron he'd been thinking it over and praying about it, and had decided to stay on. A day or two later he received a little letter from her, saying how very glad she was that he would still be her fellow-worker in Mildmay, where they served God together. He showed the letter to Bessie, who glowed with pride and affection, and said he must never part with that letter, never.

So the crisis was averted. Miss Hancock beamed, Percy's voice was heard once more singing hymns in the basement, and the hospital seemed to heave a little sigh of relief, like a giant threatened with the amputation of a foot who was told it wouldn't be necessary, after all. As for the financial ends of the Bower family that had threatened not to meet, somehow they always did meet, not only with enough to move into a four-roomed flat in Hoxton, to feed and clothe the children, but to take them away for a fortnight by the sea every year into the bargain.

In the same indefinable way the financial ends of the hospital, too, managed to tie a knot at the end of every year. 'The hospital's financial thermometer is a very delicate instrument,' the Annual Report acknowledged one year in which nearly a tenth of the total income had been raised by one Sale of Work. The income remained approximately the same for years, while the cost of treating patients slowly increased, 'due, it is thought, to a more thorough investigation of the cause of disease, and also to better and more scientific methods being used. The sick today have a much better chance of recovery than a few years ago....'

'*But it has to be paid for!*' In the 1920's patients, for the first time, were asked to pay a little, and later on a sort of insurance scheme was introduced, called the Hospital Saving Association, and those who joined knew that when they went along and presented their little green voucher, all treatment and medicine would be provided without charge. What was received from these sources, however was not half of the expenditure, and the Annual Report went on to assure subscribers that the utmost effort was made to effect whatever economies were possible.

With this claim Dr Tom Bragg's daughter Agnes, herself in nursing training at St Thomas' Hospital, heartily agreed. The utmost effort was made to effect whatever economies were possible, there was no doubt about that! Her fiancé's sister, Ruth Buxton, was a probationer at the Mildmay, and the two girls, sitting on the bed in Agnes' room, compared notes about their respective hospitals. When she heard about how paper spills had to be made to save matches, and pillow slips splitting with age were patched by the trainee nurses at the Mildmay, she groaned. Fancy having to do all that on top of your training! And the restrictions! Rules about lights being out in the nurses' home at a certain time, and not being allowed out after 10.30 p.m.!

'I'm glad I'm not at Mildmay!' said the high-spirited Agnes. 'Don't know how you put up with it!' Agnes herself had been expelled from boarding school for daring her class-mates to climb out of the dormitory window and walk round the parapet in their night clothes. She led the party herself, and all went well until, on scrambling in at the bathroom window, she found a teacher waiting.

Agnes, unrepentant and defiant, was sent home. There, on one occasion, to her father's dismay and grief, she had thrown her Bible out of the window. And although she had submitted her proud young life to Christ some time later, and was now preparing to go to China as Dr Kenneth Buxton's wife, for missionary work, she asserted that the discipline at Mildmay would be too much for her.

'I wouldn't stand it,' she said.

* * *

The years rolled on, and with them came more changes in the East End. Jews from Germany were arriving, more and more of them, bringing what they could as they fled from the rising persecution of Hitler's Nazi regime. The time came when they could bring nothing but their lives and their haunting, nightmarish memories – and an ominous sense of impending disaster that the triumphant return of Chamberlain from Munich in 1938, waving an agreement with Hitler and Mussolini, allayed for a few uneasy months.

During that time the district around Shoreditch Parish Church was agog with excitement as Her Majesty Queen Mary came to open the new Out-patients Department of the Mildmay Mission Hospital. Nurses formed a guard of honour and sang the National Anthem with gusto as she passed between their ranks. Sir George Hume, by this time Chairman of the Hospital Committee, received her, and as she went through the wards, one of the patients beamed when she spoke to him. He remembered her from her last visit, he told her, forty years ago. He'd been in hospital then, too, and she'd stood by his bed and talked to him. She'd looked out of the window, he reminded her, and,

'My! Ain't it slummy!' she'd exclaimed. Her Majesty smilingly admitted that she did not recall the incident. However, a lot had happened in the intervening years, so it was really not surprising, if she had forgotten.

Before leaving the district she paid a visit in Austin Street. Two of the residents had gone in person to Marlborough House the previous year, to present her with 70 carnations from the people of Austin Street on the occasion of her 70th birthday. Now that she was here, she said she would like to see them, so her car was stopped at the flower shop outside the hospital gates to give her an opportunity to see Mr Kite, the proprietor. She admired his shop, and bought some lilies of the valley from him.

'I hope your Majesty will always be as happy as you have made me today,' said Mr Kite, rising to the occasion with instinctive East End courtesy. Altogether it was a most successful day. The new Out-patients Department had got off to a very good start, as good as that of the largest liner in the world, the *Queen Elizabeth*, which was launched by Her Majesty Queen Elizabeth two or three months later, at Clydebank.

That was in 1938. In 1939 Bohemia and Moravia were annexed by Hitler and proclaimed a German Protectorate, Memel was ceded to Germany by Lithuania, conscription was introduced in Great Britain, Hitler denounced the Polish Non-Aggression Treaty, Britain reaffirmed its pledge to Poland, German troops invaded it on the first day in September, and two days later Great Britain entered the Second World War. The nation nerved itself for resistance. The danger would be from the air, not the sea, and London started to empty.

Under Government instructions all the patients in the Mildmay were evacuated, along with twenty-four nurses, leaving the rest of a bewildered staff manning an empty, silent hospital, waiting. . . .

Chapter Six

COMING EVENTS CAST SHADOWS

A fortnight after the outbreak of war Dr A. J. Watson took over his new responsibilities as Medical Superintendent of the Mildmay Mission Hospital, Dr White having been compelled by ill-health to retire. He came into an empty hospital, walked along deserted corridors, looked into wards with beds devoid of patients, kitchens without cooks, nurses' rooms without nurses. It was hollow and stuffy and depressing, for the patients and their attendant nurses had been conveyed to a hospital on the edge of Epping Forest, out of what was regarded as the danger zone, and what was the hospital without them? A body without a soul, vacant-eyed and purposeless. Even part of the out-patients department had been taken over as a First-Aid Post, but in those early days of the war there was no one to give first aid to, so that was empty as well.

As if to make up for the lack of humanity in the hospital, however, the Government saw to it that there was plenty of paper in the office. It looked as though there had been a long, silent process of stock-piling, for the outbreak of war unleashed a bombardment of forms to be filled in, mainly in triplicate. Dr Watson, just back from China where they had been running things differently, might well have been submerged if he had been that sort of man, but he wasn't. No record is left of the number of forms he actually succeeded in filling in, nor of those he tore up. Neither did he keep permanent note of the number of visits, letters, telephone calls he put through to the Government, pleading, demanding, arguing, all with the aim of re-opening the wards. Danger or no from air raids, the families of Bethnal Green were grimly determined to stick it out together, and when they were ill it was a hospital on their doorstep that they needed, not one in Epping Forest. The Mildmay was there, well equipped and waiting to provide them with what they needed. Its basements had been reinforced and were prepared for any emergency from the air. The hospital *must* be reopened! As for any question about putting himself and the rest of the hospital staff in danger Dr Watson's dictum 'One is always safest doing one's duty' answered that. History is silent concerning the conniving between him and Mr Alexis Jacob to obtain this end. The Annual Report for the year merely recorded,

'When it became apparent that the danger from air raids was less imminent, the Ministry of Health was approached with a view to reopening the wards. . . . Our nursing staff was allowed to return, and by Christmas the hospital was about back to normal working.' Dr A. J. Watson paced the repeopled wards, Miss Woodhouse made plans for another nursing course to start in August, and Mr Alexis Jacob returned to his home in peace.

Mr Alexis Jacob was at this time the Chairman of the Executive Committee of the Mildmay, as well as being its Honorary Treasurer. By profession he was an accountant, in private life a bachelor living with his elderly maiden sister in a tall house in Highbury, by predeliction he was a sort of financial wizard whose magic wand, when inserted into the affairs of improvident evangelical societies, dispelled the debts and produced a credit balance. He had an almost uncanny way of ferretting out old deeds, and legacies, and trusts that were hidden under stacks of paper and films of cobwebs. Like a water diviner with his twig in his hand, he walked slowly round offices, peered into cupboards long unopened, and eventually triumphantly announced that he had found a legal document that could be made to produce cash. His eyes caught the items under Expenditure that need never have been there, and the Assets which, if turned in the right direction, would produce more Assets.

Furthermore, he had the infinite patience required of those whose duties lead them to solicitors' offices and Government departments. If there was something that the cause he was sponsoring had a right to but wasn't getting, importunity based on accurate information was his line. He was perpetually turning up, complete in spats and wing collar, with his brief case containing irrefutable evidence, prepared to wait until he could see the right man. If the right man was too busy to see him today, Mr Alexis Jacob turned up tomorrow. Those who got to know him discovered that keeping him waiting was not really the best plan, for the probability was that, as he sat there thinking over his Assets, he was seeing more ways of turning them into yet more Assets. And as everybody knows, when Asset appears on one account, there is usually a corresponding Liability on someone else's.

There were those who, looking at Mr Alexis Jacob, considered that he was very old-fashioned, both in appearance and manner, and ought to keep up with the times. These opinions, expressed or implied, affected him not at all. He didn't think much of the times, and saw no reason for keeping up with them, nor going along with the crowd, either. It's the live fish that swims against the stream, and for all his high-pitched voice and unobtrusive manner, Mr Jacob was in the live fish category. When it came to matters legal he had all his wits about him. He had been on the Mildmay Committee for some ten years when the

Second World War broke out, and by this time there was nothing he did not know about Mildmay's financial affairs and legal standing. He kept a vigilant watch on estimates, the work done, and the accounts that followed, as builders soon discovered. He knew where all the legal documents were kept, and what is more, knew what they contained. He even knew what they meant. He was ready to bring them out at the appropriate moment, to the confusion of those who were making plans without due regard to the interests of the Mildmay Mission Hospital, and to the relief of those who were. What cells in the brain are to the body, so was Mr Alexis Jacob to Mildmay.

However, the young nurses could not be expected to know that.

'Wonder who that funny old man is,' thought Nurse Joan when she saw him walk along to the Administrative Offices one day. When she learned who he was. she shrugged her shoulders indifferently. Honorary Treasurers and Council Members meant nothing to her. It was the Matron and the Sisters and the other nurses with whom she had to do that mattered – especially the Sisters. The Matron was a being far removed, for whom you straightened yourself and stood back when you saw her sweep towards you, and breathed freely again when she had passed with no more than a friendly nod. The other nurses were on the same level as you were, and you could give as good as you had to take, from them! But the Sisters! They were the ones on whose reports of your progress you stood or fell, they were the ones whose penetrating glance saw when you had failed to collect the dirty tumblers, whose acute sense of smell discerned that you had forgotten to turn the gas off under the saucepan in which the rubber catheters were being sterilised, and who saw to it that when you were on duty and had done everything that needed doing in the ward, you were fully occupied with making swabs and rolling bandages, and never wasted a minute.

And strict . . . !

One day everything went wrong for Nurse Joan. Her fountain pen suddenly spurted ink and made blots when she was filling in the temperature charts, the patients all wanted something at the same time and complained at being kept waiting, she forgot to collect the tumblers, as usual, and got blamed for trolleys incompletely furnished that the nurse going off duty ought to have seen to. The day was punctuated with little scoldings, some justified but some, in her view, quite unmerited, and by the time evening came she was ready to boil over with indignation. Call this a Christian hospital! Where was the Christian spirit, she would like to know, in finding fault with every little mistake, and not seeing that she was tired beyond endurance. She reflected bitterly on the exalted ideas she had had about the Mildmay, how she had applied because she heard it was a place where nurses were trained for the mission field, expecting it all to be done in an atmosphere of gentleness and forbearance, and that faults would be overlooked and forgiven before so much as an apology had been made. Whereas, in fact, not only was there extreme strictness and discipline, but injustice into the bargain! One of the other nurses, she had observed, had made mistakes that very same day which had evoked no word of rebuke from the Sister who had scolded her so consistently. It wasn't fair! And Nurse Joan, unable to bottle up her resentment any longer, went to see the Sister about it.

'Well, you see, you're worth taking trouble over,' explained the Sister calmly. 'You've got the makings of a good nurse, and it's worth my while correcting you. She's different. She'll never make a good nurse. Her heart isn't in her work, and she'll probably leave before long, so what is the use in trying to train her?' And sure enough, a short time later the unrebuked nurse took her departure.

Nurse Joan observed these things, and meditated on them. It was borne in upon her that she was involved in the practical outworking of what she listened to with avidity and appreciation at the devotional meetings led by Matron – the clay in the hands of the potter, for instance. Clay was pummelled and pressed, slowly moulded on a monotonously turning wheel, finally placed in the shrivelling heat of the oven before it emerged as a usable vessel. Nurse Joan admitted to herself that it would be mere sentiment to glow with fervent desire in a devotional meeting, bowing the heart with the head in willingness to submit to the pressure of the Divine Potter's hands – and then to rebel against discipline because it came by way of a rather stern Sister.

Years later, surrounded by swarthy, long-haired Quechua Indians in a village dispensary in Peru, where her kitchen table had to do duty in midwifery operations, and the lives of dehydrated babies were saved through a Heath Robinson-like contraption she invented on the spot, she knew that the rugged training she had received was standing her in good stead. Mildmay had not been a place where things were made easy for you, but where you were fitted for stress and for strain, made able to endure it without breaking down. And as she saw death robbed of its prey again and again she glowed, not so much with fervent desire, as with the joy of a soldier on the field who catches the sound of the Captain's 'Well done!'

Sister Muriel arrived at the Mildmay about the same time as Nurse Joan, but being a few years older and therefore wiser had no illusions about having an easy time. She had first heard of the place a few months before, in a cinema hired by the National Young Life Campaign for a meeting where Charlie Haynes, in graphic language, told his story. She wondered what sort of a place it was, and later, receiving an invitation to consider filling a vacancy on the staff, she went along to see.

It was only after an inward struggle that she accepted the position, for Matron pointed out to her that there were spiritual demands in such a place that she would not find elsewhere. There were the ward services which required public speaking, and Sister Muriel felt clammy at the very thought of that. Then there was spiritual responsibility for the young nurses, for whom half-an-hour each day must be provided for private Bible reading and prayer, no matter how busy the wards. Over and above all there were the patients themselves, to whose sometimes penetrating questions God's answers must be given in clear and convincing replies. As Night Sister she would be expected to know how to explain to someone in distress of mind as well as body that Jesus Christ, the Lord, had died in agonising pain to give peace of heart and everlasting life to any who would place their trust in Him. It would have to be done in as simple and loving a way as possible, that the patient would be free from agitation, yet conscious of the urgency of making the right decision. Meanwhile she, the Sister, must at the same time be aware of what was going on elsewhere, so that no medical needs were neglected.

Sister Muriel, a Presbyterian from southern Ireland, faced up to these demands in a characteristically practical way, on her knees before God. She went through the events that had led up to this, remembering how she had been praying that He would show her where to go, since adverse medical reports had closed the door for her to do missionary work in China. She remembered the meeting at which she had dedicated her life afresh to God, for whatever service He required. But she had felt that she couldn't go on doing night duty. It was one of her reasons for wanting to leave the Annie McCall Maternity Hospital in south London, so what was the use of doing the same work in a hospital in the East End?

Nevertheless, the conviction only deepened that the Mildmay was the right place, so Sister Muriel accepted the position, and started duty in May, 1940, just about the time when the 'phoney war' of the early months had become the real thing to the people of the British Isles. Suddenly the calm was shattered.

The Nazi armies were sweeping triumphantly through Europe. Denmark, Norway, were occupied . . . Holland, Belgium, Luxembourg. . . .

The King, supported by the Archbishop of Canterbury, called for a national day of prayer, and crowds flocked into the churches that Sunday. . . .

The B.B.C. news broadcasts daily announced withdrawals of the British Expeditionary Force in France under heavy fire. . . .

The boys were retreating towards the coast. . . .

They had their backs to the wall – but the wall was the English Channel, with twenty-five miles and more of water between them and the homeland. . . .

It all culminated in a crazy conglomeration of ships and yachts, tugs and rowing boats, 3,500 of them, moving across towards the French coast, as England rallied all her resources to save her sons, massing on the beaches of Dunkirk.

Britain succeeded in rescuing 355,000 of them, bringing them across waters that were fantastically calm. The courage and the loyalty displayed on that first day of June turned a disastrous retreat into a national epic – but even the most materialistically minded had to admit there must have been a cause not human for the amazing stillness of the proverbially choppy Channel, and the umbrella of mist that concealed it. Some people remembered the day when the nation had prayed.

Sister Muriel followed the course of the war as best she could, along with everybody else at the Mildmay, but there was little enough time to meditate on it. The nation had been left in no doubt as to what the next few years must hold – blood and sweat and toil and tears was what Winston Churchill promised them, and the country prepared to resist invasion. The evacuation of school children from Greater London began in earnest, and whole families moved into the country.

For the most part the East Enders of London stayed where they were, even if it did mean sleeping in the Underground railways and the air raid shelters, coming up in the morning to look at new desolations wrought by bombs, and spit back defiance in their Cockney way.

BUSINESS AS USUAL

Wreaths to:	Bouquets to:
Hitler and his gang	R.A.F.
	A.R.P.
	A.F.S.

appeared on the blinds over the blasted out windows of Mr Jones Kite's flower shop at the corner of Austin Street one morning, and the Mildmay staff chuckled appreciatively. Trust the Kites to come up with the appropriate answer, whether with courtesy to queens or with insolence to Nazis!

The hospital, staff and patients, got into the habit of disappearing into the bowels of the earth as evening approached, the honeycomb of corridors and rooms in the basement becoming thick with beds, while nurses slept on the shelves in the linen rooms. Morning after morning those on duty emerged, not knowing what they would see, and morning after morning, going the rounds of the place, breathed a sigh of thankfulness to see how little damage had been done to the buildings.

'The Mildmay's the safe place,' the Air Raid Precaution men said, and reckoned themselves fortunate when they were stationed there. 'It's a good billet,' they said, especially when Sweet Apple Square with its factories and warehouses was razed to the ground, while the hospital which adjoined it remained practically intact.

'Can't understand it – never seems to get hit,' people would say. 'Had an incendiary bomb or two fall on the roof now and then, but the fire watchers always got 'em in time. Very lucky! Good people they are in there, very kind to the patients. Very religious, of course. Prayer meetings and all that. They say God protects them. Well, I don't know about that. Not a religious man myself. But it makes you think. . . . It makes you think. . . . '

Meanwhile, the normal ills to which mankind is heir even in times of peace continued unabated, and in the end it was the bronchitis, not the bombs, that brought Mr Tom Brooks into Mathieson ward as a patient. The hospital committee was mildly surprised that he had asked to come to the Mildmay.

'After all he's said about us!' was the wry comment of those who for many years had heard his acid comments and endured his broadside verbal attacks against hospitals that introduced religion. Mr Tom Brooks, was a local celebrity. He had started his working life as assistant to his father, a chimney sweep, and knew quite a lot about the ramifications of those dark, horrifying passages between the fireplace and the chimney stack, up which trembling little boys were sent to loosen the soot. He had become a master chimney sweep himself in the process of time, but being a public spirited man had taken a hand in local politics as well, with such success that he had become the Mayor of Bethnal Green. As such, his avowed distaste for the Mildmay, where there was hymn singing and praying in the wards, Bibles by the beds, and texts on the walls, had often made things difficult for the hospital committee. Now, in his old age, plagued with bronchitis, he had actually chosen to come to the Mildmay! What was the reason for it?

If the young nurses who had heard about him thought that he had chosen to come because his views on religion had undergone a change for the better, they soon discovered they were mistaken. Lying back on his pillows he took a delight in cleverly involving them in arguments about their faith from which they emerged defeated, while the other men in their beds, listening to it all, winked at each other with amusement. After a time others took part in this baiting of the nurses, and one night Nurse Joan, trying to concentrate on her duties, was peppered with so many questions from her patients that she told them to write them down and she'd deal with them all at once, when she led the ward service before going off duty.

She regretted doing this when, after a night on the ward, she was confronted with a long list of questions of the Why-does-a-God-of-love-let-people-suffer variety. She got as entangled in trying to answer them as a kitten in a ball of knitting wool, and retreated from the ward almost in tears, feeling a complete failure and utterly unsuitable to be a missionary.

But the bronchitis was gaining on Mr Brooks, and it was this fact that got him in the end. He'd had to come into hospital several times, and one day he said to Sister Muriel,

'I can't understand it. I keep having treatment, and yet I

seem to be getting worse. Why is it?'

Now Sister Muriel was a very good nurse, and a sympathetic one, too. She might have tried to comfort him, to reassure him, to console him by saying that he was really doing very well, and he'd be out again very soon, and it was wonderful what medical science was doing in these days. But Sister Muriel was also a simple, honest person who was prepared to give a straight answer to a straight question. And she knew Mr Brooks had asked a straight question, that he was in earnest, and not 'larking'.

'Well, you see, Mr Brooks,' she said kindly, 'you're not getting any younger. You're getting older. You have this bronchitis every year, and it's getting worse each time.'

It could scarcely have been more simple, or more self-evident. Mr Brooks looked up at the broad-cheeked, blue-eyed, earnest little face above him, and the full force of that self-evident fact struck him for the first time.

He was getting older. The bronchitis was getting worse. The time would come when the bronchitis would win, and he wouldn't be able to breathe, and the gates of death would open, then shut again, with him on the other side.

With him on the other side. Cut off for ever from all the familiar things of this life, from the streets of Bethnal Green, the buses and the evening paper, from the convivial society of friends and home, even from this old body of his that had life in it now, but wouldn't when he couldn't breathe any more.

And Mr Brooks was afraid. All those quips and clever arguments that got the young nurses tied up in knots, those if-there's-a-God-why-is-there-so-much-evil-in-the-world sort of questions that they tried in vain to answer, faded right out of his mind as he faced the inexorable, self-evident fact that one day he must die.

It was a fact that couldn't be argued against, and it reduced him to silence – and submission.

What other mysterious influences were brought to bear upon the soul of Mr Brooks that day it is impossible to say. Perhaps it was the accumulated evidence of the texts and the singing, the preaching and the kindness, and the attitude of those young nurses who were beaten in argument but whose unshakeable confidence in what they seemed unable to prove was the greatest proof of all. Perhaps, behind all this, Someone Whose existence he had so vehemently denied was silently revealed to him. Whatever it was, as far as Sister Muriel was concerned the next thing she knew was that Mr Brooks was looking at her with tears in his eyes, and asking rather shakily,

'What can I do to become a Christian?'

It was another straight question, and Sister Muriel gave him another straight answer. It didn't take long, for it was very simple. The One Who could transform the dark terrifying doors of death into the mere valley of a shadow was right there, ready to take him on with never a word about all those years of defiant unbelief, ready to give him a free passport, as it were, into the realms not of darkness but of everlasting light. As for Mr Brooks, all he had to do was to accept it – here and now. Did he want to do so?

In some ways a hospital ward is as good a place as any other for such transactions, but it does have the disadvantage of lacking in privacy. Lack of privacy is especially trying to the Englishman, who prefers not to show his feelings except when he has them well under control, and the Mildmay, of course, made allowances for this. The nurses could cut off a patient from view in a trice, sweeping the cubicle curtains round his bed, leaving nothing to be seen but their own black-shod feet.

Sister Muriel's feet often told a story. When the student nurses saw the curtains being swished quickly round a bed, and then saw Sister Muriel's feet, soles up, protruding from under them, they knew what was going on. Sister Muriel was on her knees by the patient's bed, praying. Sometimes they were told what she had been praying about, and sometimes not.

In the case of Mr Brooks, however, not only the nurses were told, but the patients too, and that by Mr Brooks himself. He'd come to Christ, he told them, and he made no attempt to argue himself into a good position over it. He had come in simple faith, and Christ had accepted him, in spite of all the wrong he had done and said – particularly said. The change in him was so marked that everybody noticed it, and the news got round the hospital in no time – 'Mr Brooks is converted!'

About the same time another old man was admitted, a quiet friendly old man, but evidently as indifferent to Christianity as his friend Mr Brooks had been opposed to it. After he had been in for a few days, however, he explained the reason why.

'I'll tell you my story, if you can spare me five minutes,' he said to Sister Muriel. He went on to explain that when he was young he had believed in God, and had promised Him he would be a missionary. 'Then things went wrong. Gradually, I turned my back on God. I got farther and farther away.' Life had been no more easy for him than for many another, and as he recounted his troubles she said,

'I'd have thought these things would have made you realise your need of God.'

'No, they only made me harder. But now. . . .'

He paused a minute, staring straight in front of him, and then went on,

'Now I'd give anything to have peace with God. But it's too late. I've gone too far . . .'

'But it's not too late,' said Sister Muriel eagerly. 'That's the glory of the Gospel – there's a way back to God! There's a way back to God! He's a God who forgives. . . . ' She had plenty of evidence for that in the Bible, from King David who committed adultery and betrayed a loyal soldier to death, to Peter the disciple who denied his Lord. But Mr Rogers could not be convinced. He shook his head sadly. He'd gone too far – it was too late. Sister Muriel had to hurry away in the end, and leave him.

A few hours later a piece of paper was handed to her.

'Mr Rogers asked me to give you this,' she was told, and opening it she read,

'Sister Muriel, Jesus has found me and I found him through Hymn No. 222 in the small hymn book. Heart too full for words.

'At 6.35 p.m. Mr Rogers.'

It was this sort of thing, when it reached the ears of Mr Alexis Jacob, that made him rub his hands together with glee and apply his mind with renewed diligence to the account books and the legacies, the deeds and the documents that related to the Mildmay Mission Hospital. This hospital must be kept open and it must be kept open on the right terms. Its position must be safeguarded legally. It must be free to do this sort of spiritual work as long as there were workers ready and able to do it, and its right to do so must be made perfectly clear. And it was his duty to ensure that this was done.

Mr Alexis Jacob plunged into dark labyrinthine passages of old reports and minute books, legacies and Government papers. He turned up tomes and unearthed papers over which he pored earnestly until a gleam came into his eye and he made notes on his pad. From time to time that rather egg-like forehead of his, from which the hair was steadily receding, bent low over his desk, and his eyes closed. Those who knew him realised that in those moments Mr Alexis Jacob was entering another realm. He entered that realm frequently.

And he entered it in the correct way. Mr Alexis Jacob was not one to blunder in anywhere. He liked to be sure of his ground. He might be kept waiting outside the doors of officialdom when making his applications, but they had to open to him in the end because they were the right doors, and he knew it.

It was the same when it came to approaching the One on whose shoulders all ultimate authority rests. There are those who rush into prayer on a flood of passionate feeling. Others embark on it confident that they have a good case. Mr Jacob, however, deliberately drew near to God on one basis only. As far as himself was concerned, he had not a leg to stand on, no merits to plead. But since it was clearly stated that through His death Jesus Christ had opened a way whereby penitent sinners were invited to come to God and make their petitions known, he took full advantage of that privilege. He found that after he had done it, not only was his mind at rest about the matters he had mentioned, but that in often imperceptible ways things worked out for good, and that he himself got some new ideas on which to go on working.

There were times when the full significance of those ideas only became evident years later. It was so in the case of the trust deed.

It was while the air battles over Britain were at their height, with the island kingdom as Europe's only hope of deliverance from Nazi rule, that the need for a deed in which the objects of the Mildmay Mission Hospital were clearly defined was forced upon the mind of Mr Jacob.

The immediate reason for this was that the Annie McCall Maternity Hospital was to be offered to the Mildmay.

Annie McCall had founded her hospital in 1889. An intrepid young woman, she had struggled to obtain her M.D. against odds which would have been too great for most of her sex. The medical students among whom she was the only woman may have been perfect gentlemen when in Victorian drawing rooms, but they were anything but gentle in the lecture halls, deliberately trampling back on Annie's toes so heavily that she soon learned to wear shoes with the thickest leather uppers she could obtain. But she had won through that, and a good many other things, too, including the widespread use of alcoholic stimulants in medicine and the high mortality rate in maternity. Her methods spoke for themselves when it was proved that in her hospital the mortality rate was 1.6 per thousand while the national figure was 4.51.

Now she was in her eighties, however, and felt the time had come to hand the hospital over to some organisation with the same aims and ideals as her own. In any case, it was closed, for it had been bombed so heavily in September 1940 that it was uninhabitable. The Mildmay Mission Hospital had been approached, which explains the absorption of Mr Alexis Jacob with the matter of drawing up a Deed, so worded that there could be no doubt about the purpose of the hospital. His excursions into the papers of the past led him to what he was looking for.

'To heal the sick and to diffuse simple Gospel truth.' There it was in the original Trust Deed of the William Pennefather era, delightfully clear and uncomplicated, and Mr Jacob scanned it to his entire satisfaction. In ten short words the position was made plain, and it was unnecessary to add anything. The words were incorporated in the Deed, which passed through the various processes required to satisfy the requirements of Government and Law, Charity Commissioners and Trustees, and emerged like pottery that has gone through the oven, with the words like a pattern indelibly inscribed. When it was eventually returned, Mr Alexis Jacob saw that it was lodged in a very safe place.

Did he realise how far-reaching would be the effects of that carefully prepared Deed? Did some Divinely implanted instinct warn him that it would be of vital importance in years to come? Was he rather like an old warhorse, who 'scents the battle afar off'?

Probably nobody knows. The immediate effect of the Deed was to put the Mildmay Mission Hospital in a position to make the humble request that Her Majesty the Dowager Queen Mary become the hospital's first patron, to which she graciously acceded; and to incorporate the Annie McCall Maternity Hospital.

Mr Alexis Jacob had done what was necessary, and could now turn his attention to other matters, like looking into the fading finances of the Foreign Missions Club, a hostel for missionaries on furlough, and preparing for his weekly Bible Class in Highbury, and, of course, his periodical visits to play cricket with the boys at Bethnal Green. Playing cricket with the boys at Bethnal Green was always an important item in his diary – and theirs. When he emerged with his bat and took up his position at the stumps, they spat on their hands, rubbed them together, and crouched with knees bent, ready for the leap or the run. They were on their mettle. This opponent, for all his prim, old-fashioned appearance, was not to be taken lightly. They knew that when their best bowler sent the ball hurtling down the pitch, Mr Alexis Jacob, as likely as not, would hit it for six.

Chapter Seven

CRISIS

Nurse Edna ought to have been in bed. She had been on night duty, along with three or four other young nurses, and the middle of the morning usually found them all on their beds, trying to sleep. On this particular day, however, she had decided to go out first, to get some air and do some shopping. The others had followed suit, so they were all in the street some distance from the hospital when they heard the sound of an aeroplane overhead. A single aeroplane in the sky was no uncommon thing – but when its engine suddenly stopped it meant trouble. It was 1944, the era of the deadly flying bomb which was killing civilians in their hundreds, and filling the hospitals with casualties. In-patients were being sent home at the earliest possible opportunity or evacuated from the thickly populated areas to make room for the victims of the aerial attacks against which there seemed no defence.

'It's a doodle-bug!' Everybody cowered, in the streets, in the shops, in the houses, instinctively trying to shield their heads as they waited for the terrifying blast they knew would follow the silence. Nurse Edna cowered, too. She had been in this sort of thing before, standing at a bus stop one minute and finding herself flattened against a wall thirty yards away the next. She had escaped with a few bruises that time, and when she lost her voice a day or two later she knew it was only the result of shock, and she'd soon get over it. But what would happen this time?

She held her breath, and waited. Where would the bomb fall?

When the sound of explosions and crashing masonry subsided, and the whining of ambulances and police cars took their place, Nurse Edna and her companions started to run.

'The noise came from Shoreditch!' they panted. 'The hospital . . . !' Anxiously they threaded their way through the streets, where people were clawing at the crumbling buildings and heaps of rubble, the splintered glass and the nightmarish array of doors, furniture, buckled bicycles and vehicles that had been hurtled together by the blast; clawing, clawing, trying to get at the bodies. . . .

'The steeple's still there!' Nurse Edna gasped thankfully as they came within sight of Shoreditch church. The Mildmay Mission Hospital clock chimed the hour. '*And* the old clock!' The people in the streets around listened for that clock. The sound of its half-hourly chimes brought them a sense of security in a tottering world. If anything went wrong with the clock Percy Bower was up its tower like a shot, to put it right. He knew what its bells meant to lonely old women and frightened mothers when the droning of planes and the roar of explosions had died away. 'The Mildmay's still there!'

The Mildmay was still there this time, too, but a battered, sightless Mildmay with its windows blown out, its front doors out in the courtyard, lying amongst the bunches of flowers and wreaths that the blast had carried there from the Jones Kite's shop, along with bricks and slabs of concrete and broken window-frames. What a shambles the place looked! Poor Matron!

It was not the damage that was done to the building that mattered to Matron Woodhouse just then, though – it was fear of what had happened to those young nurses who had come off night duty and who, as she believed, were up on the top floor of the nurses' home. As soon as she realised that this was the part of the hospital that had received the greatest damage she sent the porters up there.

'The night nurses! They'll be in bed. . . . Quick, quick!' But the night nurses were not there, though it took the men some time to discover the fact, for their rooms were a debris. The only one who had been in bed when the blast went off was Nurse Joan, and she was occupying a room in another part of the building, from which she emerged somewhat bewildered that her Ovaltine tin had shot out of the window but had scattered its contents all over her. She did not know where the other nurses had gone.

When, a short time afterwards, Nurse Edna and her companions turned up, running in from the wrecked streets, Matron Woodhouse slipped into the short, informal thanksgiving service for which Dr Watson had called. He had looked out of his window after the blast to see a deep crater where previously the ground had been level, and to observe with awed amazement that the hospital, perched now on what looked like the top of a precipice, was nevertheless intact. What she wanted to give voice to was her relief and gratitude that her girls were not among the maimed, battered bodies even now being laid out in rows on the mission hall floor.

As for the night nurses themselves, of course, they went straight back on duty. Throughout the whole of the day and on into the night they followed the doctors around as they gave their terse instructions, passing slowly between the rows of casualties.

'Morphia for this one. . . .'

'Morphia. . . .'

'No use – can't do anything here . . . Pass on . . .'

'Morphia for this one. . . .'

'Gone . . . Cover her up. . . . Mortuary. . . .'

On it went, hour after hour, the thin stream of battered humanity coming into the hospital, some on stretchers, some supported by friends, to sit in a dazed, bewildered way on chairs around the wall, or lie on mattresses on the floor, so blackened with smoke and dust, some of them, that they were unrecognisable. Later started the long queues of people who had been searching among the ruins for those they loved, and had not found them. Had they been brought to the Mildmay? The lists were scanned time and time again, and when the search proved fruitless and the enquirer turned heavily away, even sympathy had to be controlled, for there were others waiting.

The Allies might be gaining ground in Europe, but during those days and nights of 1944 the sound of a single aeroplane overhead was the warning of death and destruction to the people in the British Isles. Nevertheless, the end was in sight. The tide of the war had turned, and almost daily now there was news of fresh advances, cities retaken, and prisoners liberated. The BBC broadcast stirring eye-witness accounts of the exploits of Field Marshal Montgomery's troops and the crossing of the Rhine. Then the news flashed round the world that Mussolini had been executed by Italian partisans . . .

That Himmler had offered to surrender to Great Britain and the U.S.A., but on terms that were rejected . . .

That Hitler's death had been announced on German radio. . . .

That the Germans had surrendered unconditionally.

London heaved a great sigh of relief, almost too exhausted to get wildly excited. The war in Europe was declared officially over at one minute past midnight on May 8, 1945, and three months later, with the capitulation of Japan, the Second World War came to an end.

London celebrated in typical fashion. Bonfires were lit all over the place, and the people of the East End swayed along the pavements singing,

> *'Felix kept on walking . . .'*
> and
> *'Hang out the washing on the Siegfried Line.'*

en route for Buckingham Palace to cheer the King. The crowds who elected to celebrate nearer home surged around the streets instead, their peregrinations as consistent as those of Felix, shouting their derision at the Siegfried Line until Edna, Night Sister by this time, felt she was on the shore of a sea whose waves beat with relentless regularity on her ear-drums.

As far as she was concerned, a pall set over the festivities about 10.30 p.m., when all the young probationer nurses who had been allowed out by Matron as a concession to patriotic feeling were supposed to be back indoors. Sister Edna had been told to report if any had not returned by 11 p.m., but here it was, past midnight, and three of them were still missing. She was torn between her sense of duty towards Matron and her desire to shield the merry-eyed Eunice and the two who were with her. They could look after themselves all right, she had no doubt about that, but what would she say to Matron when she took her her morning tea at 6 a.m. if they had not returned? How would she face those reproachful eyes, and answer the question, 'Why didn't you let me know?'

She was spared the ordeal by their arrival, on very sore feet, at about 4 a.m. They were dead tired, they said, but it had been worth it. The King and the Queen and the Princesses had come out on the balcony again and again in response to the shouts of the crowd, and the singing of 'For he's a jolly good fellow,' and 'Auld Lang Syne'. Even the diminutive Eunice had seen everything, since she'd been hoisted up by the other two. But their expectation of being able to get a taxi back to the hospital had been ill-founded, and they'd had to walk all the way through jostling crowds, cheered on by the policeman who noticed them staggering up Ludgate Hill and called out, 'Never mind, girls! The first twenty miles are the worst!' They were dying to get off their feet, and have a cup of tea. . . .

Sister Edna's eyes were glacier-like, and she made it plain she was not interested. Her voice cut like scissors through the frivolous fabric of their reminiscences as she faced them with cold reality. Matron did not know they had not returned at the stipulated time, she having perjured her soul to defend them, and if Matron ever found out . . . ! They'd better get up to their rooms as quickly and as quietly as possible, and as for sore feet, they'd be expected to be back on duty sharp at 8 a.m., feet or no feet. The war was over, but the hospital was still going on! Matron did not know they weren't in by 11 p.m., she reiterated, but if ever they were late again she, Sister Edna, would make it her business to report to Matron at once.

The war was over, but the hospital was still going on. Sister Edna turned smartly on her heel and made for the wards, while the three culprits crept meekly up the stairs.

What none of them realised was that now the war was over, the hospital probably would not go on.

* * *

It was early in 1942 that Dr Watson had informed a Council Meeting of the Mildmay Mission Hospital that he had heard that the Government was planning the post-war co-ordination of all hospital services. With all that the Government had on its mind it was remarkable perhaps that it had any time at all to give to post-war planning of hospitals, with the end so far away and the outcome so uncertain. And with so much to do in the hospital, with shortage of staff and difficulty in getting supplies, and the perennial problem of making ends meet, it is equally remarkable that Dr Watson had any time to write an article on the subject of that post-war planning, and how it could affect the Mildmay. The writing of articles was not much in his line – it was in the writing of prescriptions that his talent lay. The clouds over the far horizon of the end of the war that were indiscernible to the layman's eye, however, appeared ominously before that of the Medical Superintendent. A warning note had been struck. A debate in the House of Commons in April made it clear that something was brewing, and a survey of the work of each hospital in the Greater London area brought it to the boil. Dr A. J. Watson took up his pen.

Although nothing had yet been decided, he explained, it was clear that the Government was making plans for a National Hospital Service to be brought into being after the war. '. . . it is possible that should a hospital be found to be redundant, or not up to the standard expected, or too small for economical running, its continued existence will be doubtful.'

The article went on to say that the survey of Mildmay having been made, there was nothing to fear on the first two counts, but there was ground for anxiety on the third. The hospital was a very small one. There were only fifty-four beds, and it was generally recognised that a 100-bed hospital was a more economical unit than one half its size. For this reason, 'its continued existence will be doubtful'.

Dr Watson went on to explain that the Mildmay Council, alive to the need for enlarged premises, had during the last decade acquired property adjoining the hospital, and one of the bombs from which the hospital narrowly escaped destruction had, in fact, demolished the factory buildings, leaving it a splendid site on which to build an extension. Nevertheless, no widespread appeal for funds would be launched while the war lasted. That would be unfitting. 'The very existence of our Christian Faith is at stake, and the needs of our country take precedence over everything else.' The Government must wait until the end of the war to put its plans into operation, and so must the Mildmay. The friends of the hospital were being told the situation now for one reason only – that they might pray. Nothing else was asked of them – only prayer.

To what extent the subsequent events were due to those prayers it is impossible to assess. Who prayed, how earnestly they prayed, how much faith they brought to their praying, is beyond human knowledge to assert. As well try to trace every little stream, every drop of rain, every hidden spring that goes to build up the right volume of water on which a vessel can pass through before the lock gates are opened.

Whoever did or whoever did not pray, however, it is certain that Mr Alexis Jacob did. He had been present at the Council Meeting early in 1942 when the matter of the nationalisation of hospitals came up, and with that ability of his to see beyond the hills of present difficulties, he realised that as far as the Mildmay was concerned the danger of demolition from enemy bombs was small compared to the danger of demolition from a benevolent Government. The mountains in the distance that were wreathed in clouds to those absorbed in the present stood out sharp and clear to him.

If all the hospitals were nationalised, the distinctive character of the Mildmay would go. No longer would it be a training ground for missionary nurses. No longer would it be a place where the Gospel of God's Grace was freely proclaimed twice a day in the wards, once a day in the O.P.D., and any time of the day or night anywhere where a soul was found in conscious need of it. Nationalisation would mean standardisation – unless God did something about it.

Unless God. . . .

If God still had a use for the Mildmay Mission Hospital, then He could do something about it.

What would He do?

How would He do it?

Mr Alexis Jacob did not know, but he could not believe God had no more use for the Mildmay Mission Hospital. Not while there was a stream of Christian young women applying for nursing training so that they could go to 'heal the sick and diffuse simple Gospel truth' not only in England, but in other lands, too. Not while there were patients emerging from the Mildmay healed in soul as well as in body. Not while there were men like Dr A. J. Watson in the consulting rooms and Percy Bower in the basement, working together to run the hospital in a way that would be a credit to their Master.

No, Mr Alexis Jacob could not believe thatGod had no more use for the Mildmay as a Mission Hospital. And since each one in it had an appointed task, and he seemed to have been set on a sort of spiritual watch-tower to watch, that is what he did, biding his time.

Meanwhile, things continued as usual in the hospital itself. The magazine that was produced every three months gave reports of comings and goings, of the meetings held, news from former Mildmay workers in mission fields overseas, pen pictures of happenings in the wards, and suggestions of ways in which well-wishers could help by their contributions of cash and of pretty well anything in the way of furniture, old clothes, down to tin foil. The Appeals

Secretary, to whom all gifts should be sent, would put them all to the best use. The Enquiry Officer, or Almoner, went to and fro to find ways in which patients in material need could be helped. Patients came in sick and went out healthy.

'Such a lovely happy spirit everywhere,' they said, ignorant of what went on behind the scenes, with the Sisters demanding such a high standard from the probationers that every now and then, depositing the dirty clothes they had carried down to the basement, they turned the buckets in which they had brought them upside down, sat on them and had a good cry. Percy, arms akimbo, would shake his head as he looked at them, and try to cheer them up. As father of a family himself, he knew what they needed.

'It's hard now, but it'll be worth it,' he assured them. 'You'll be glad you've gone through with it later on.' Then, lowering his voice a little, he would add,

'I'll tell you what I'll do, only don't mention it. I'll put the clothes in the boilers for you and run the water on – just this once!' He knew it was against the rules, but it was worth taking a risk to get those wet eyes dry again, and those little pink noses restored to a normal colour. As for the Sisters, what with the food rationing, and having to economise with every little thing, and see to it that the ward services were maintained, and that all the patients were properly looked after, no matter what happened, there were times when they would have been glad to subside on an upturned bucket and have a good cry themselves.

On the other hand, of course, there were times when merriment prevailed, and ripples of laughter eddied and flowed.

A letter had been delivered addressed to the Mildew Mission Hospital!

A small patient, arguing about having a whiff of gas again before a minor operation, asserted that he'd get a gastric.

An older one, in reply to the doctor's greeting, replied, 'Oh, Doctor, I'm afraid I'm a chronical bronical!'

And in the magazine itself, a solemn article which concluded with the words, 'God is not willing that any should perish; this is the Divine economy, and this, cost what it may, must be our aim,' was followed by a notice in big bold lettering

DON'T FORGET WE STILL NEED TINFOIL!

It is doubtful whether the probationer nurses so much as knew that the Government, during 1944, had published a White Paper, in which its health proposals were set forth for discussion. The Sisters probably did, and the Matron certainly. But it was Dr Watson, the Medical Superintendent, Sir George Hume, Chairman of the Council, and Mr Alexis Jacob, Chairman of the Executive, who read it through as those who must nerve themselves for action. They had already been faced with a sharp increase in expenditure as the full effect of the Rushcliffe scale of salaries was felt for the first time. Although donations to the hospital had increased by more than £2,000 during the year, legacies had fallen below normal. The Hospital Savings Association provided nearly £4,000 of the hospital's income, and contributions from patients for services rendered, £1,500. The main bulk of the income, however, came from other sources, and the total expenditure of the year, at £16,392, fell £853 below its income.

The Annual Report for the year covered various subjects, and only one paragraph was devoted to the White Paper.

'In spite of the assurance of the Minister of Health that he desired the continuance of the Voluntary Hospitals in the post-war scheme, voluntary hospitals as a body viewed the White Paper proposals with some misgiving. For this hospital in particular, any measure which might lead ultimately to State control and therefore to a curtailment of its evangelistic and missionary enterprise, cannot be regarded without anxiety. . . .'

The same report also contained the Annie McCall Maternity Hospital matters.

The battered building had been occupied by the Lambeth Borough Council as a wartime day-nursery, so there were no in-patients at all. Its total income was £1,920, and it had a credit balance of £15 at the end of the year. Altogether, the prospect of the two hospitals, united on paper but widely separated geographically, mustering as many as 120 beds between them was remote. And in view of the Government's ideas, which were in the process of crystallising into plans, and thence into laws, how would the little East End hospital stand?

Now that the war was over the Government, that powerful giant, was applying its mind to many matters, like who should have the atomic bomb, and whether the U.S.A. could be tapped for a loan. The Government did things on a big scale, and when it talked of National Health it talked in terms of hospitals with thousands of beds, of gathering up all small ones into a sort of sausage machine and turning them out fewer but bigger and better hospitals. It talked of municipal hospitals and voluntary hospitals all in one breath, of building up those that were in 'key' positions and lopping off the rest, so that eventually the smallest hospital in London should have no less than 700 beds, to be run by the Government and supported by the taxpayer. As for schools of nursing, they must be dealt with in a similar fashion. The time had come when things ought to be standardised, all brought under one head, and then kept up to the mark.

The Executive Committee of the Mildmay, which made it a point of honour to know what the Government was talking about when it came to hospitals, held its breath. At the rate things were going, the Mildmay might be swept away in a flood tide of new legislation, its staff scattered, its texts cast on the rubbish heap.

Donors got wind of the dangers. One lady of strong convictions, who wished to endow a cot in memory of her sister, wanted first to be assured that the money would not fall into the hands of the Government if voluntary hospitals were nationalised. Other donors followed suit. The Executive Committee was in a quandary.

Meanwhile, Dr Watson decided to go and see the Government itself, to present his case and plead the cause of a hospital which stressed the training of medical missionaries. The Government of course, is a many-limbed giant, and Dr Watson approached what might be termed the local limb. He went complete with last year's financial statement, which mercifully was a good one, and a list of the hospital's consultants whose standing obviously ranked high. The Government's local limb was friendly and encouraging, expressed the opinion that because of its missionary training the Mildmay would probably be regarded as a special case – and added that it might be linked with The London Hospital in Whitechapel.

The Executive Committee breathed a little more freely for a time. But the undertone of anxiety persisted. When Dr Watson was asked by visitors representing a fund which contributed generously to hospitals what was his greatest concern, he admitted it was lest the Mildmay should not be allowed to retain its status as a training school for nurses.

Only a short time after that visit, the blow fell.

During the war the General Nursing Council had decided very reasonably that in the post-war period it would not recognise as a training school for nurses a hospital with less than an average of 70 occupied beds. On this basis the plans for extension at the Mildmay had been drawn up, although there was little immediate hope of putting the building in hand. But now the G.N.C. requirements had undergone a change, and only a hospital with an average of at least 100 occupied beds would be considered as a training school. This was to take effect in May, 1947.

It looked like the end, as far as the Mildmay was concerned.

Chapter Eight

THE FORT IS HELD

The news that the Mildmay Mission Hospital was too small to be registered as a training school for nurses, and would cease to be in that category after May, 1947, had a more disturbing effect than any of the war-time bombs. Dr Watson and Miss Woodhouse knew very well what the steady intake of young women with a sense of Christian vocation meant to the life of the hospital. Without them its whole character would change, if, indeed, it could exist at all. As for the young nurses themselves, they felt as though the path they had been treading so confidently had suddenly led them to a trackless desert.

'But what shall we do?' they asked anxiously. 'How shall we finish our training?' Some of them were in tears. 'Will all these months we've spent here be wasted?' No one could answer their questions, and it was obvious that no one had a solution to the problem.

'There is nothing we can do – but God can help us. Let us pray to Him. Let us see what He will do,' said Miss Woodhouse. She arranged that for half an hour every evening, at 9 p.m., when the nurses came off duty, the dining room should be open for any who wanted to go to pray about the future of the hospital.

Night after night they crowded quietly into the dining room, their faces very earnest and anxious. Night after night they gave voice to their desire, pleading that God Who had called the Mildmay into being and provided for it in so many wonderful ways, and so remarkably protected it all through the war years, would step in now and meet this new crisis on their behalf. What they wanted more than anything else was that the training school for nurses should not be closed down. It seemed impossible now for it to continue, but they went on praying.

It meant so much to them. Their expectation of becoming State Registered Nurses had been based entirely on getting their training at the Mildmay. For several of them its emphasis on preparation for medical missionary work had been their reason for applying in the first place. It was a major crisis in their young lives, and they could do nothing about it. They had come to Mildmay because they believed God had sent them, and now there was this block in the way, this apparently unsurpassable block – Oh, God, reveal Thy power! They were desperately in earnest.

Then, gradually, a change came. The situation remained the same, but the note of anxiety subsided in those evening prayer meetings.

'Where is our faith?' the young nurses asked themselves. 'God is more concerned about Mildmay than we are. It's *God's* work. Think of all the nurses in missionary work who got their training here!'

'And the doctors who came here to do their houseman's year, and then went to mission hospitals!

'Yes. It's God's work. Look at the patients whose lives are changed – ever so many of them have come to Christ. . . .'

'It's God's work, and we're praying about it. What's the good of praying if we don't believe He'll answer? It's wrong for us to be worried!'

'It's wrong to be worried. We're told in the Bible not to be anxious about anything, but to pray about it, and believe God will hear. That's what it says, so let's stop worrying and start believing!'

Meanwhile, ideas were beginning to formulate in the minds of those who knew that if the training school were to continue, they themselves would have to act. Its future might well depend on what they did *now*. The question was, what could they do?

Miss Woodhouse, in her narrow little sitting room only ten feet from the clanking of the lift and the constant sound of footsteps mounting and descending the stairs, gave herself to thought. She faced the fact which lay behind the apparent inevitability of the closure of the schools.

The hospital was too small. It could not provide nurses in training with all the experience they needed. It lacked facilities with which they ought to be acquainted. It was ideal as a training ground for day-to-day nursing, but when it came to specialised work in the operating theatre, and in the wards, dealing with every branch of medicine and surgery, they could not get it in the Mildmay. It was in the larger hospitals that such experience was to be obtained. If only the Mildmay nurses in training could go to one of the larger hospitals for that experience, while getting their general experience in the Mildmay, all the requirements of the General Nursing Council would be met.

Would one of the larger hospitals open its doors to provide such experience and training?

Her thoughts went to The London Hospital which, in various ways, especially during the war, had shown a big brotherly interest in the little Mildmay. She remembered occasions during the war when provisions had been sent over from the bigger hospital to help meet an emergency in the smaller one. The London Hospital! If one had a medical problem one could always turn to The London. If one needed a piece of equipment, one could always ask about it at The London. And had not the Government itself, in the person of its local limb, suggested the possibility of Mildmay being linked to The London?

The day came when Miss Woodhouse, always meticulously dressed, adorned herself with special care, fastened her pince nez firmly on her neat little nose, patted her snow-white hair under her modest but good quality hat, and took a taxi to Whitechapel Road. She had an appointment to meet the Matron of The London Hospital, to discuss schools of nursing. . . .

The outcome of that interview was a scheme which, after being submitted and scrutinised, stamped and sealed by all the appropriate authorities, enabled the Mildmay Mission Hospital to continue as a school of nursing, associated with The London Hospital. The Mildmay would accept the nurses for training, and be responsible for them throughout. For specified periods of time they would be transferred to the London, but return to the Mildmay taking their finals as Mildmay nurses.

That this privilege was granted was remarkable. There is no doubt but that the particularly good record of the Mildmay nurses (97% in the final exams), had a lot to do with it, added to the fact that there were very few who did not complete their training, and there was always a long waiting list of applicants. The type of work to which so many of them went told in its favour, too. They were nursing, and training others to nurse, in under-developed countries. Nevertheless, it was a hospital with only fifty-four beds. As it happened, there were plans for extension which had been held up on account of the war, and without these it is doubtful whether the Government would have let it continue, in spite of all that could be argued in its favour. Weighed in the balances, however, it was decided there was sufficient evidence to justify the tiny hospital continuing as a school of nursing. The delicate transaction was carried through satisfactorily, and the young nurses were told they could continue their training.

The news came like a reprieve to them. God had quietly worked on their behalf, in answer to their prayers, of that they were sure. Some of them were delighted at the prospect of a few months at The London, though others viewed it with mixed feelings, reluctant to leave their cosy little hospital by Shoreditch Church for the big unknown one in Whitechapel. They all wondered who would be the first to go, and when they heard, they chuckled.

'Have you heard? It's to be Olive – and the Colonel!'

'The Colonel!'

'Yes. Nora Vickers. The Colonel herself. The right one to do the pioneering for us, isn't she?'

Nora Vickers herself was not so sure, though she squared her shoulders and set about her preparations in a business-like way. She had become accustomed to finding herself in unusual situations. When she had been called up, during the war, a few weeks of nursing had made her decide that she detested it, and would have to find some other form of war work. As far as she could discover, there were now only two choices before her.

1. She could become a tram conductress.
2. She could apply to go to India as a FANY.

FANY, she learned, was an organisation that had been started after the Boer War by well-to-do ladies who planned that a team of horsewomen should always be at the ready in the event of another war, to go on to the battlefield to tend the wounded. By the time the 1914 war broke out horses were on the way out, so the FANYS became ambulance drivers instead. When that war was over the FANYS held together as a voluntary corps, worked as drivers during the General Strike, and when the Second

World War broke out they offered their services to the Government which took them on to do coding, deciphering and administrative work in the War Office.

Now the War Office said it needed fifty FANYS in India, and there were not fifty FANYS who could go. Hence the need for recruitment of the right type of young woman to become a FANY – no longer as a voluntary worker, of course, since the young able-bodied but unqualified voluntary worker had followed the horse off the stage, but as a salaried member of an organisation which still retained a high position in society. All FANYS were given officer status.

Nora Vickers went before the selection board, was accepted, fitted out with a smart khaki uniform, and shipped off to India. There she was put in charge of the Officers' Mess in Calcutta, with thirty-five women under her. It rather took her breath away!

She came to the turning point of her life in India. She might easily have been carried along in a gay social round, for there were plenty of opportunities, with about one hundred young officers to one FANY. Nora was of a serious turn of mind, however, and hearing of the Officers' Christian Union, went along to the meetings and joined the Union, the only woman among them.

It was here she realised for the first time the implications of discipleship. Being a Christian was not a mere matter of church attendance and abstaining from the more obvious forms of evil and wordliness. 'If any man will come after me, let him deny himself, take up his cross, and follow me,' Jesus Christ had said. He had followed that up by asserting that the one who tried to save his own life would lose it, but the one who was prepared to lose it would save it. Obviously He was referring to daily living, not to the battlefield, and Nora saw the point.

One of the things that was evident was that the people who did deny themselves pleasures and luxuries that others accepted as their right, who cast their personal ambitions aside when they conflicted with what they believed their Master required of them were, in fact, much more vital and deeply satisfied than those who went through life pleasing themselves. She saw that the principle of losing the life to save it worked, even in Time, She could have no doubt that it worked in Eternity.

Nora Vickers started out on the road of discipleship. She had not travelled very far before the matter of missionary work came before her. 'I believe God is calling me to go to China as a missionary,' she said.

Hard on the heels of that conviction came a less acceptable one. The subject of nursing came up again – that detestable job! Everything seemed to point to it, however, as being the best way she could prepare herself for a life in a remote part of the world, far from medical facilities.

'You ought to go to the Mildmay Mission Hospital,' she was told by an elderly couple in the Civil Service with whom she had become friendly. 'It's a fine place, especially if you want to become a missionary nurse.'

'I've never heard of it,' replied Nora. 'Where is it?' They told her. They had been there as patients during their last home leave. 'That's the place for you,' they asserted.

When the war ended, therefore, and she returned to England, she promptly arranged to go to see the matron, walking smartly into the hospital in her full official regalia, unconscious that she was earning for herself a nickname that was to stick throughout her training days – 'The Colonel'!

However self-possessed the Colonel may have appeared, she came away from that interview feeling as though she had been turned inside out and found wanting. It was all very awe-inspiring after Army life in Calcutta. The frail-looking Miss Woodhouse, with her innate dignity, perfectly modulated voice and well-chosen words, asked quite unexpected questions, culminating with,

'What is the answer to the need of the human heart?'

Nora tried not to look alarmed. She was not accustomed to people talking like that.

'Well – prayer. . . .'

Miss Woodhouse waited.

'And reading the Bible, of course . . .'

Miss Woodhouse waited.

'And we need to go to church,' Nora faltered on. 'Worship . . . fellowship with other Christians. . . .'

Her answers tailed off into silence.

'Yes,' said Miss Woodhouse, 'But all these are works that we do, aren't they? They won't answer the need of the human heart.'

Nora was being driven back to fundamentals, and she found it hard to define them. She had not been called upon to do so before. What was the answer to the need of the human heart, with its inherent fear of the Unseen and the uneasy awareness that its own craftiness and lust and pride must one day be exposed for Judgement? She gulped, then blurted out,

'I don't know of any other answer but tomorrow.'

It would have been no answer at all had it not been that the following day was Good Friday. Nora was unable to express herself clearly. She had never been called upon to articulate her faith before. She only knew, rather dimly, that the crucifixion of Jesus Christ was what brought relief from her sense of guilt.

'I don't know of any other answer.'

Miss Woodhouse nodded. 'My dear, there is no other answer,' she said quietly. There was silence for a few moments, then she went on,

'And do you feel you will be able to take your share with conducting and speaking at the ward services?'

Again Nora tried not to show her alarm.

'With God's help, I could,' she said breathlessly.

The interview terminated with Miss Woodhouse praying that God would guide them both, and Nora departed. She would not suit the Mildmay Mission Hospital, of that she was sure. She was not surprised to receive a letter from Miss Woodhouse suggesting that she should train somewhere else. 'So that's that,' thought Nora with relief. Now she could apply for training in a hospital near home. A couple of days later, however, another letter came from Miss Woodhouse, saying there was an unexpected vacancy for a nurse trainee, and Miss Vickers could come at once.

Nora did not want to go. The place had oppressed her. She was sure that she would not fit in – she wasn't the right type. She could never talk about things the way Matron did. She had not got the right background for that sort of phraseology.

However, the conviction that she ought to go was so strong that she went. She was demobilised by this time, and had parted from her officer's uniform for ever. She entered the hospital one Saturday evening, lugging her suitcase, to be confronted with a text on the wall. 'The Lord shall be thy confidence,' she read, and wryly said to herself that nobody had ever needed it more than she did now! She felt overwhelmed by the austerity, the rules and the timekeeping. Being a probationer in the Mildmay Mission Hospital was a very different thing from queening it in the Officers' Mess!

'Look at the Colonel!' said one of the nurses with a chuckle as Nora, carrying two buckets of rubbish, made her way down the stairs to the basement. Nora grinned rather feebly as she went on. She had deposited the rubbish, and was filling two buckets with coal when another young nurse came hurrying along the basement corridor.

'I've been sent down to get something and I don't know what it is,' she said breathlessly. She went into Percy's workroom. 'Sister sent me down to get something,' she said looking round in a bewildered way. 'Something that sounded like pork and beans.'

'Pork and beans? That's a Balkan Beam you want,' said Percy cheerfully. 'There it is, indicating the traction apparatus. Nora, returning to the ward carrying two buckets of coal, realised that this nursing job, which she was not enjoying very much, had its lighter side.

It certainly had its heavy side. You reported for duty on the wards at 7 a.m., and were hard at it until 9 p.m., with half an hour allowed for each meal, and a couple of hours free in the afternoon. 'I learned what constitutes a good day's work at Mildmay,' she said many years later. 'So when I was a missionary I expected to work like that – and to do it without feeling sorry for myself!'

She learned something else, too.

'I soon found out that Christians are not perfect. The staff at Mildmay had their faults, like everyone else – yet I could see that God was using them. It taught me to accept people as they are, and it saved me from a lot of disillusionment later on. And a great thing about Mildmay was the way the patients were treated.' They always came first.

The patients spoke to her about it. 'Mildmay's different,' they often told her. 'You're a *person* here.' That was something different from being merely a body with a pain in it. 'They care about you yourself! Don't send you off the minute the wound's healed. Want to make sure you'll be all right when you've got home. And the way they look after you! Take Mr Brown there,' Nora glanced across the ward. A man whom she knew had a perforated gastric ulcer was lying back on his pillows, watching the nurse who was going from bed to bed with a medicine trolley. 'Take Mr Brown there. At death's door he was, time and again. But Sister Muriel . . . Well, she just wouldn't let him die! Ha! By his bedside day and night she was. Wouldn't let 'im die. And now . . . '

Mr Brown's voice was heard, speaking slowly to the nurse with the trolley.

'He's orf that medicine now, nurse!' he said. 'The doctor's put 'im on penicillin. . . . ' Mr Brown had been in the ward so long, he was almost like a staff nurse!

For Nora the transition from the homely little Mildmay to the great London Hospital was nearly as drastic as had been that from administering the Officers' Mess to cleaning the wards. It was not only the vastness of the place, either. The uniform of the Mildmay nurses was slightly different from the others, and there was evidently something else that marked them out.

'You Mildmay nurses are so damn cheerful at breakfast,' complained one heavy-eyed damsel irritably one morning. It was not the sort of complaint Nora had ever heard at Mildmay, where grievances were of a different nature, and aired more quietly. The Sister whose probationers had one day hurried thoughtlessly into the ward and vigorously dusted everything had managed to convey a chastening rebuke by silently appearing with the broom and doing the neglected sweeping herself.

It was when Nora found herself nursing in the surgical ward for patients who had had very intricate brain operations that she realised the advantage of experience in a big hospital. Miss Woodhouse realised it, too. She had viewed the departure of her nurses with many misgivings, but as time went on it became evident that association with The

London was providing them with knowledge and ability they could never have gained at the Mildmay. The new arrangement, brought about by something that had threatened the very life of the hospital, was being turned to its advantage.

There was another matter that was weighing on her mind, however. The Health Services Act had been passed, and before long would be put into operation. The days of Mildmay's independence were running out. Notice had been given that the hospital would be taken over by the Government and would come into the jurisdiction of the North East Metropolitan Regional Board. No longer would the staff be appointed by the Mildmay Mission Hospital Committee. No longer would the personal faith and Christian experience of an applicant be of prior consideration. The question that arose time and time again in the mind of Miss Woodhouse was whether, in the new order of things, the preaching in the wards would continue, with that 'diffusion of simple Gospel truth' which was the very breath of life in the hospital. Would it continue to be the Mildmay Mission Hospital – or would the 'Mission' be lost sight of, and gradually disappear altogether?

Miss Woodhouse, her mind at rest about the nurses' training, was still uneasy. She knew she was approaching the end of her own life of service at the Mildmay. She had been appointed matron when a comparatively young woman, in 1919, and had remained there ever since. Her own knowledge and experience was limited almost entirely to what she had been able to obtain in this one small hospital. Now that the National Health Service had come into operation and the Mildmay was no longer an independent voluntary hospital, her type of matronship would pass away.

A woman with higher academic qualifications, and who was accustomed to moving in the workaday world of men and affairs would be appointed to take her place. Miss Woodhouse accepted that. She had served her own generation after the will of God, according to her ability, and her own generation was passing away. The questions she continually asked herself as she looked into the future of Mildmay under that unknown matron of the new generation were:

Will she keep the ward services going?
Will she ensure the nurses have their half an hour for quiet, alone with God, every day?
Will she be concerned for the spiritual well-being of the patients as well as their physical health?

She did not know who would take her place. In the old order of things she would have had no anxiety, for she would have known the Committee would not appoint anyone whose Christian convictions were not the same as theirs and hers. The old order had changed, however, and the Mildmay Mission Hospital Committees no longer had authority to appoint staff. The fulfilment of the aim 'to heal the sick' would take priority over the second, 'to diffuse simple Gospel truth.' The new matron herself might decide to wash her hands of that which Miss Woodhouse had held most dear – that which she referred to as 'the spiritual side of the work'. If so, what would happen, and how would the simple Gospel truth be diffused?

She thought and she prayed and she thought again. If Matron did not make herself responsible, who would see to the ward services, and the Bibles placed on the lockers, and the personal talks to people in spiritual perplexity? Miss Woodhouse pondered the matter, and somehow came to the conclusion that it would all continue very well indeed if the same people who were doing it now went on doing it. She thought of Sister Muriel Jameson in Mathieson Ward, and of the men she prayed for, and nursed, and wouldn't let die – men who went out of hospital firmly announcing they had found Christ there. She thought of Sister Edna and her care for the younger nurses, and the unfailing regularity with which the ward services were held when she was in charge, no matter how busy things were. If Sister Muriel and Sister Edna were in the hospital, she had no doubt about the diffusion of simple Gospel truth.

So Matron had an interview with the two young Sisters, and told them what was in her heart. She knew she could not go through with all the changes that were coming in with the National Health Service, and that she would have to go. She had come to the age to do so, though she and they knew she would have stayed on if things had remained as they were. What was worrying her was lest there should be no one to carry on the spiritual side of the work. What she wanted to see them about was to tell them that she believed they were the ones to do it, and to ask if they would stay on at Mildmay, to tide things over during the change-over. She did not put it exactly in those words, but what she was suggesting was that they should be like the pistons in an engine, holding things together as the wheels continued to revolve.

They were both amazed. *They* be responsible for the spiritual side of the work? Such a thing had never entered their heads. For as long as they had been in the Mildmay it had been Matron in whose hands that lay. No Mother Superior of a convent was regarded with more awe and respect by her young novices than was the Matron of Mildmay by her sisters and nurses. That they, mere Sisters, and young ones at that, should receive such a charge took them completely by surprise, and for Sister Edna, at least, it brought her to the first of a series of crises which resulted in her still being in the hospital a quarter of a century later.

The crisis on this occasion was that she had to reconsider the whole matter of the Sunshine Home for Blind Babies. She was in the process of applying for the job of matron of the Home, and knew that she stood a very good chance of being appointed. She loved babies, and blind ones made a special appeal. On the more practical side, she would have her foot on the ladder of promotion. If she remained at the Mildmay, she would have to take her foot off that ladder.

She did not give her reply to Matron immediately. She had to think about it – and pray about it. And as she thought and prayed, she remembered. She remembered applying to a missionary society because she wanted to go to China as a missionary. Her offer of service had not been accepted at the time, and the reason she had come to Mildmay in the first place was that she wanted to obtain nursing qualifications and then try again to go to China. She remembered how she and Lucy Clay, in training at the same time as she, had prayed together about the Fanling Babies Home in Hongkong. She had applied to go as matron of that, and when her medical reports were seen, it was decided her health was too hazardous, and again her offer of service was not accepted. Lucy Clay went instead.

Sister Edna remembered all this, and as she thought and prayed about what she should say to Matron, she came to her decision. She prayed to God to nerve her to do what she knew was right, even though it was not what she wanted, and went to Matron and said,

'I wanted to be a missionary, but the Lord closed the door. If He's opening it for me to help train other young women to go to the mission field, instead of going there myself, then I'm willing to stay on at Mildmay for this time.'

By 'this time' she meant the transition period that lay ahead. After the new matron had been appointed and things had settled down again, then she would be free to move out into another stream. She did not know then that the next time she started to apply for a different appointment another crisis was to arise and that again adherence to a principle was to be the deciding factor convincing her that Mildmay was still God's place for her. It happened again and again until, twenty-five years later, and with retirement from nursing beginning to appear over the horizon of her life, she herself was saying, re-echoing the words that had been spoken to her,

'We must secure the future spiritually. Many changes are coming in nursing and the system. We must ensure that there is always someone doing the spiritual work here in the Mildmay.'

Chapter Nine

SECURING THE FUTURE

The passing of the National Health Service Act in 1946 threw the voluntary hospitals and medical clinics into a turmoil. In most cases they had a religious foundation, and many were the discussions, the committee meetings, the prayers and the appeals which ensued when the much contested Act was finally passed.

Shall we continue as we are, and not join in the Government scheme? If we hold out, where will the finance come from, were some of the questions asked? The raising of funds by public appeals had been the chief means of financing them, and now that Government was to provide hospitals free, would people be prepared to contribute to the upkeep of private ones? Many of the voluntary hospitals had introduced their own insurance schemes, with people making the small, regular contributions which entitled them to free medicine and hospitalisation when they were ill. With the Government's own insurance scheme imposed on the nation, would people be likely to continue paying in to their own local hospitals as well?

The answer to those practical financial questions soon became obvious in the case of the Mildmay Mission Hospital. The missionary societies which looked to the Mildmay for medical help when their workers were in need of medical care or surgery were unable to undertake any adequate financial support, and no other organisations could be expected to do so. There were a few charities which made regular donations to the Mildmay, but their contributions fell far below what was required to run a hospital. In fact, if it were not taken over by the Government, the Mildmay Mission Hospital would soon cease to exist at all. Other hospitals, with the backing of wealthy Roman Catholics or Jews might continue independently, but not the Mildmay.

Inevitably there were those who insisted that this attitude was one of unbelief, not of faith, and that since the silver and the gold are God's, as well as the cattle on a thousand hills, He could as easily provide for the Mildmay's needs without voluntary contributions and insurance schemes as with them.

And He would! Was He not still the God of Elijah! Was the day of miracles over? God could provide, and for the glory of His own Name, He would provide!

This argument is one always difficult to contest in theory, and equally difficult to support in the face of unpaid bills. 'That He can provide in miraculous ways none of us doubts. That He will choose to do so, we are not so sure,' was the answer given many a time in private, if not in public, when the subject came up for discussion – often quite heated.

Those who had conducted Mildmay affairs for many years, and had been observing the trend of things, were of the opinion that it was not so much the Elijah-like expectation of dramatic Divine intervention that was called for as the courage and the faith, the determination and the integrity of a Nehemiah. To run a Christian hospital in the National Health Service would require as much faith and prayer, and as much help from God, as to run one independently. Perhaps more. To obtain the right sort of people on the staff might well prove to be as difficult in the days to come as had it been to obtain the money to pay the bills in the days that were past.

For it was evident that more than ever the distinctive, evangelical character of the Mildmay Mission Hospital was going to depend on obtaining the right staff – and at the right time. The Government would naturally and rightly demand adequate medical and academic qualifications in those appointed. The Government would not enquire into the religious convictions or private lives of the applicants. It would not be the Government's business to do so. If an important position had to be filled, then the one who had the right qualifications would be appointed, whether he was an evangelical Christian or not; he might be an atheist or a Muslim, as far as the Government was concerned. The Government would not quibble over matters like that – indeed, in a free country, it would be exceeding its duty if it did so. What mattered to the Government was that the hospital, medically and in administration, was up to the standard required.

People like Dr Watson and Mr Alexis Jacob followed what was happening in Parliament very, very earnestly in those days when the Health Service Bill was being discussed at committee level. Many were the letters and representations from people of strong religious convictions that were received and sorted out, filed and responded to by the committees. The Roman Catholics* were particularly importunate, and it was largely due to the pressure they exerted that, as clause after clause was added to the Bill, one was added in which Dr Watson and Mr Alexis Jacob saw a ray of light.

There it was, if somewhat ambiguous, at least providing something on which to make an approach to authority.

* It is interesting to note that after the Bill was passed in Parliament, most of the Roman Catholic hospitals elected to remain independent.

Clause 61 was its number, and it read:

'Where the character and association of any voluntary hospital transferred to the Minister by virtue of this Act are such as to link it with a particular religious denomination, regard shall be had in the general administration of the hospital and in the making of appointments to the Hospital Management Committee to the preservation of the character and association of the hospital.

On the strength of this Dr Watson and Mr Alexis Jacob took counsel together. All non-teaching hospitals were to be grouped under various hospital management committees, they knew. These committees in turn were to be responsible to regional boards. They had been informed that the Mildmay would be one of the hospitals in the Central Group of the North East Metropolitan Group, and would be managed by this body. No longer would the Mildmay Mission Hospital Committee have authority to make senior appointments. That would be the responsibility of the Group Management Committee.

Thus the old order was changed with the stroke of a pen, although the nurses tripping up and down the wards scarcely gave it a thought, if they so much as knew about it. What they were concerned about was whether their patients were improving in health, and what hymns to choose for the ward service, and how to proclaim the Gospel in a way that would be both fresh and clear when it came to their turn to do the speaking. And what the two men poring over Clause 61 in the new Act of Parliament were concerned about was that those young nurses should always have the liberty to do just that. The future for that proclamation must be secured.

Mr Alexis Jacob was not baffled by the sixty-two word

sentence which comprised Clause 61. He was accustomed to legal documents devoid of terminating punctuation. He studied those sixty-two words carefully, and saw that one of them was of special significance.

Preservation. That was the operative word.

Preservation of what?

The preservation of the character and associations of the Hospital.

What were the character and associations of the hospital?

Mr Alexis Jacob had his argument ready, couched in the clear and simple language of that Trust Deed. How vitally important had that Trust Deed suddenly become! There the aims of the Mildmay Mission Hospital were outlined – in nine words, the longest of which contained seven letters.

'To heal the sick and diffuse simple Gospel truth.'

Furthermore, although that Trust Deed only dated from 1943, it was based on the first Mildmay Trust which was registered in 1873. Mr Jacob had all his evidence, ready to contend to the death that the Mildmay Mission Hospital had had the aim of healing the sick and of diffusing simple Gospel truth from its inception.

Probably feeling not unlike David with his sling and his five smooth stones, Mr Alexis Jacob, supported by Dr A. J. Watson, set out to confront Government, armed with the Memorandum and Articles of Association, and ready to explain the nature of the Trust Deeds.

The particular limb of the Government giant they were to meet was the Secretary of the Regional Board. He received them courteously, and listened attentively as they explained their case.

The Mildmay Mission Hospital, in spite of being in one of the most heavily bombed areas in the British Isles, had functioned almost without remission all through the war, and its fifty-four beds were steadily occupied.

There was a waiting list of young women wanting to come in for training as nurses, the consultants who held their clinics in the hospital stood high in their profession.

The number of out-patient attendances during the past year was 34,779, while 922 in-patients had been admitted.

Financially, its budget balanced.

The Secretary nodded appreciatively.

Then they went on to outline the manner in which the daily work was conducted, with short services in the wards morning and evening, periodical services in the Mission Hall which patients who were well enough to do so were free to attend. Since there had always been an emphasis on preparing young people for medical work as missionaries overseas, the Medical Superintendent must be one who himself had been a missionary doctor.

Having given all the information that seemed necessary Mr Alexis Jacob, never one to waste time on the perimeter of things, plunged to the crux of the matter.

He referred to Clause 61 of the National Health Act. He emphasised particularly the words about 'the preservation of the character and association of the hospital'.

In view of this Clause, he enquired, how were the character and associations of the Mildmay Mission Hospital to be preserved?

What means would be employed to ensure that the aim of diffusing simple Gospel truth, as well as of healing the sick, would be fulfilled?

How could the character of the Mildmay Mission Hospital be preserved if the people appointed on the staff were those whose apprehension of Gospel truth was embodied in the sort of personal reminiscences which ended with the words, 'and what I'm telling you is gospel truth'?

If he did not express it in exactly those words, there was

no doubt as to what he meant. And the Secretary saw the point. The position had to be made clear.

In the first place, the Mildmay Council had been divested of authority. It was no longer responsible for the Mildmay Mission Hospital nor for the Annie McCall Hospital in south London, either. Authority for the Mildmay Mission Hospital was now reposed in the Central Group Board; and that, of course, included appointing senior staff.

However, the Secretary had something else to say. He recognised the hospital's right to preserve its character. When the Regional Board appointed a Hospital Management Committee, the Mildmay would have representation. That being the case, it would be up to those representing it to convince the Committee of the reasonableness of their requirements – and that included convincing the Committee of the suitability of their staff nominees.

Mr Alexis Jacob and Dr A. J. Watson came away from the interview satisfied but sobered. That assurance of Mildmay representation on the Hospital Management Committee of the Board was the best that they could have hoped for. It gave the opportunity to nominate candidates for staff appointments. But how much was going to depend on those Mildmay representatives, and their ability to convince the other Committee members that their nominees were suitable!

And what if there were no committed Christians with the right qualifications to nominate when vacancies occurred? How could they secure the future?

They knew they could not do so. They had done all that lay within their power to keep the door open for those who would follow them when the time came to relinquish their responsibilities at the Mildmay. 'Our times are in Thy hands', the Psalmist had written nearly three thousand years before, and it was the same today. There was some satisfaction in the knowledge that they had, as it were, stuck a foot in a closing door, and kept it ajar. Whether it remained ajar, or closed altogether, would largely depend on the standard of work in the hospital itself, and in the right people being on hand at the right time. Medically, as well as spiritually, it must be a good hospital if it was to continue as a fruitful field for evangelism, a place where the evangel of the love of God was freely proclaimed.

As for the Annie McCall Hospital, they could do nothing about it. Unlike the Mildmay, it had been badly bombed during the war, and all efforts to re-open it and get it functioning effectively again, had failed. It would now come under the South West Metropolitan Regional Board, and its future would be linked with the South London Hospital for Women. So at the same time as the Articles of Association, owing their existence to the acquisition of the Annie McCall Hospital, saved the future of the Mildmay, the Annie McCall, with its still unsolved problem of becoming fully functional, was taken away.

* * *

The Appeals' Secretary was winding up her department.

She herself had been in charge of it only two years, but it had been an integral part of the hospital from the beginning. There had always been letters to write to donors, and arrangements to be made for meetings and sales of work, and for many years now there had been the magazine to be edited and distributed as well. It involved addressing a lot of envelopes as well as addressing a lot of meetings. The task of the Appeals' Secretary had been to create interest in the hospital, interest that would result in financial support from the sort of people whose own desire was that it should 'heal the sick and diffuse simple Gospel truth'. And Mary Stockton had taken it all on with enthusiasm.

It had involved a good deal of getting out and about to meet people, as well as office work. She now seemed to know personally many of the people who contributed regularly, like the old age pensioner who sent ten pence in an envelope twice a year, or the well-to-do married couple who covenanted to give an annual £100 apiece for seven years. She knew the people who acted as local secretaries, distributing the collecting boxes made in the shape of beds, then organising special 'Box Opening Days' periodically, at which their contents were publicly disclosed, and the grand total of copper and silver coins duly handed to a representative of the Mildmay Mission Hospital. Mary Stockton herself, as Appeals Secretary, was often enough that representative, and she entered into all the behind-the-scenes arrangements thoroughly, as well as being the official speaker at the meeting itself. It was a varied life, and she experienced all the feelings of mingled anxiety and exultation known by those responsible for the finances of an organisation that exists on voluntary contributions. She had seen, during her two years in office, the remarkable timing of donations and legacies arriving just when big bills were due for payment, and had rejoiced at seeing the balance being turned from debit to credit. She had heaved many a sigh of relief when an ordinary-looking envelope was opened to reveal an unexpected gift, and realised that it had come after her somewhat urgent prayers for more money. Some of those experiences had been thrilling, bringing an awareness that Someone she knew but had never yet seen, the Lord of Creation Himself, had heard her prayers for the little East End hospital of which she was now a part. It was something quite beyond anything she had been taught during her training as a hospital administrator.

When she had applied to the Mildmay Mission Hospital

to work in the Appeals Department there had been those who said she was being very foolish, and that with her qualifications she could get a much better job. She realised that as far as promotion was concerned, she was not aiming high. But there was one very important element in the matter that she could not ignore, and that was the very deep conviction that God wanted her there.

She was not one who readily asserted, 'God told me to do this' or 'God led me to do that'. Others might be very sure about what God was telling them to do, but not Mary Stockton. Perhaps her knowledge of human nature in general and her own in particular made her uneasy lest personal inclination should be mistaken for Divine guidance. When it came to replying to that advertisement for an assistant in the Appeals' Department of the Mildmay Mission Hospital, however, she was very definite. God wanted her to apply, and the fact that her application was accepted and she was appointed seemed to her to prove it. The Mildmay was God's place for her. Addressing public meetings was not what she had been trained for, nor writing articles for magazines, nor organising flag days either, but she found herself doing them all in the course of her duties, and enjoying them, too.

It was people's love for the hospital, and their enthusiasm in supporting it, that made her work so rewarding and enriching. She could not but respond to it. There was the earnestness of the ladies who held sales of work which they and their helpers had been steadily preparing for for a year, making something out of nothing to sell on behalf of the hospital. There was the eagerness of the patient from the Midlands who 'fell in love' with the hospital and organised a 'Mildmay week' in his town to raise support. (The Appeals' Secretary had taken a missionary on furlough, formerly a Mildmay nurse, to address the round of meetings he had arranged.) Then there was the readiness of factory owners and shopkeepers and publicans in the neighbourhood of the hospital to have collecting tins and boxes of flags on sale for the Mildmay Flag Day. 'Glad to do anything for the Mildmay' they said. And as for the response of people to the little magazine articles written in story form about the need for a certain piece of furniture, or curtains, or towels – well, it was positively exciting! There was something in those human little stories about homely little needs that never failed to strike a sympathetic chord in hearts. Hands went into pockets, and the wards suddenly flourished with something fresh, colourful and useful, to the surprise and delight of the patients, the appreciation of the nurses, and the gratification of the Appeals' Secretary.

But now all that sort of thing would soon be over. The people who all through the years had been sending money to support the hospital, who had responded warmly and often self-sacrificially to special appeals, must now be discouraged from doing so. The Mildmay Mission Hospital which had depended on their support now needed it no longer. The Government was taking the hospital on, complete with its assets and its liabilities, and the Government would be responsible for paying all the bills.

In one way, of course, it was going to be a great relief. The need for all the economies, and the contrivings to make a little go a long way, the delays in putting in an order for something that seemed essential in case it could not be paid for, would no longer be necessary. All the same, it was not without a sense of sadness that the Appeals' Secretary closed the books and walked out of the hospital on that historic day in 1948. It was the end of an era.

She would walk in the next morning at the usual time, and go to the same office, sit down at the same desk. The building would remain the same, the staff would be unchanged.

But it would all be under new management. She would be employed. not by the Hospital Committee with Mr Alexis Jacob in the chair, but by the Government, represented by 'The Group'. The old days of tension when finances were low, turning into blessed relief at the appearance of legacy or large gift, were over. The prayer meetings for funds, those prayer meetings when they had come like children to a Father, asking foı such strangely mundane things as new X-ray equipment, or fresh quilts to replace the dingy, darned ones in the nurses' home, were over, too. (As things turned out, there were going to be many opportunities to pray about the mundane in the days ahead, but Mary Stockton could not know it then.) Would the sense of belonging to one big family, working together without any thought of only doing so many hours a week, have to go too, she wondered?

She would have to keep strictly to time, she resolved, and ensure that everything she did in office hours came into the category of service as a Government employee, called Administrative Secretary, not as a member of the staff of a voluntary evangelical hospital. 'Render unto Caesar the things that are Caesar's' must be her attitude in office hours. It was going to be a matter of keeping things in time-tight compartments, and the forms that the Government demanded to be filled in, and the committees that the Government demanded must be attended, and the reports that the Government demanded must be scanned, would have to occupy her days, along with the multitudinous matters ranging from dealings with the rag and bones man to escorting high officials round the premises, that fell to the lot of an Administrative Secretary.

Therefore the production of the magazine, and the

letters to friends of the Mildmay, and the going away to speak at meetings, and all the things that were bound up in maintaining that precious relationship with the people who loved the hospital must be done out of office hours. For it had been unanimously agreed that the people who loved the hospital simply could not be cut off. Dr Watson and Mr Alexis Jacob and all the members of the Council which now found itself without any authority at all, were agreed on that. To be divested of legal authority over the hospital they accepted, but for the hospital to be suddenly bereft of all those friends who sent in gifts, and took an interest in its activities, and prayed for the patients and the staff so earnestly and lovingly, they could not bear. The poor little hospital would be like a lamb shorn of its wool and left alone in a keen east wind, without them. It did not need their money now, but it did need them.

'In fact, it is doubtful whether the hospital can preserve its evangelical character without them,' the Council privately observed. 'If there are not praying people now, people whose prayers in the name of Jesus can change men and change circumstances, this place will never survive. We *must* keep our praying friends.'

The question was, how to keep them? As the Council thought round the matter, and prayed about it, a solution was found right within themselves. It was the League of Help.

The League of Help was quite a small affair – a group of kind-hearted ladies who had heard pitiful tales of patients too poor to go away for the convalescence they so greatly needed, who had returned to their dreary impoverished homes to lose all the strength that they had gained in hospital. Something must be done, said the ladies, and they formed themselves into a League of Help, to provide amenities for the very poor patients, and to pay for them to go to convalescent homes.

If a League of Help, why not a League of Friends? A League of Friends banded together to pray for the work of the hospital, to support the evangelistic activities, and to provide on a more extensive scale for the after care of patients – this was the way to retain the love and interest that would otherwise gradually be lost.

So the League of Friends was formed, registered with the Charity Commissioners as a Limited Company, with Mr Alexis Jacob as the chairman, and Miss Mary Stockton as the secretary. The magazine continued to appear as usual, but as the organ of the League of Friends of the Mildmay Mission Hospital, and the epoch-making change-over from being a voluntary hospital to one that was State-controlled was made with so little fuss that most people did not realise when it happened.

The staff knew, however, and wondered what it would mean for them. From being a little independent unit the hospital was now part of a great machine, like one small cog in a wheel, with Ministries to deal with – and Unions. Percy the Porter knew very little about Unions, but he did know they sometimes instructed their members to go on strike, and the very thought of anyone in the Mildmay going on strike was enough to silence his song in the basement. Apprehensions were nicely balanced by evident advantages, however, such as a rising scale of salaries, and as time went on fears subsided. There were difficulties and new restrictions, but none were insurmountable, so long as Caesar's things were rendered to him.

One day the Government sent its auditors to the hospital, and sitting in the Administrative Secretary's office, drinking coffee with her, one of them fingered the magazine, and glanced through its pages. In it he noticed a brief report of an afternoon meeting at which she had spoken on behalf of the League of Friends. The auditor enquired,

'Do you do this sort of thing as part of your office duty?'

She had not expected the question, for it had not occurred to her he would even see that article. But the question was simple enough for her to answer,

'Oh, no,' she said. 'That isn't the Administrative Secretary's job. I just happened to have a half day due to me, so I took it at that time so that I could attend the meeting.'

Caesar was satisfied.

Chapter Ten

THE CHANGEOVER

The first noticeable change on the staff of the Mildmay was the new matron. She had not been reared in the Mildmay tradition, as was evident from one look at her fashionable hats and the suggestion of make-up on her face. Nor did she conform to the Mildmay pattern of a matron, whose qualifications had always included that of an eloquent preacher. The successor of Miss Dora Woodhouse (who had spoken at more of the hospital services than anyone else), came from that branch of the evangelical community which discourages women from any public utterance in the Church. The contrast could scarcely have been more striking, yet the fact is that basic beliefs are the same. The new matron was an evangelical.

As it happened, she was also an accomplished musician. With unfailing regularity and a quite unself-conscious humility, she took her place at the little organ instead of on the platform for the services held in the mission hall. Without questioning anything they did, she left Sister Edna and Sister Muriel to ensure that the ward services were carried on just as before her appointment, that there were Bibles by all the beds, and that the nurses had their half-hours each day for quiet.

Her invaluable contribution to the hospital was in the nursing administration. It was she who introduced nurses' study days, appointed a permanent tutor, opened a well-equipped nurses' demonstration room, arranged with consultants to give lectures, and generally raised the training standards so that by the time she left in 1956 the hospital was in very good standing with the General Nursing Council. The old order had changed, but God had His servants ready for the new. No longer was a matron to be at the Mildmay for a lifetime. It is worthy of note, however, that the three well-qualified women who successively occupied the post were all evangelical Christians, and all came to the hospital with a strong inner compulsion that God was sending them to it. The rapidly changing pattern in the nursing world inevitably resulted in more frequent changes in the personnel in the hospital.

It is therefore all the more remarkable that while, by 1972, nearly all hospitals but the psychiatric units had dispensed with their medical superintendents, the Mildmay continued to have one – and one not only whose professional qualifications were such as to satisfy the Government, but one whose record as an evangelical missionary satisfied the requirements of the Mildmay House Committee. That body, divested of legal authority, continued to exercise its right to preserve the character of the hospital.

In 1952 Dr A. J. Watson was overdue for retirement, but no one had been found to take his place, and as far as the Government was concerned, no one was needed. Medical Superintendents were on the way out. It took some persistence in public and prayer in private to persuade the Government that in the case of the mission hospital its unique character required one. Eventually the Government agreed, and all that remained was to produce a suitable person as nominee for the position; which was not so easy.

The matter of a successor to Dr Watson was lying in what might be termed the 'Awaiting Attention' file in the mind of Mr Alexis Jacob one day early in 1954, as he walked along the Strand from his office. There were several other matters in that mental file, of course, such as the fortunes of the Foreign Missions Club, which had undoubtedly looked up since he had taken a hand in its affairs. Also there was his weekly Bible class at Highbury, where his housemaid's niece and also her husband had recently firmly announced that Jesus Christ was now their Lord, much to the joy of his housemaid, as well as of himself. Furthermore, the League of Friends of the Mildmay Mission Hospital was preparing to launch out with a new venture in the shape of a convalescent home. As Chairman of the League he was deeply involved with this. The prospect of providing a place where the good work of healing body and soul, commenced in the hospital, could be rounded off, was further brightened by the knowledge that it would be in the voluntary category.

All these, and other matters, were in his current activities, so as he threaded his way along the crowded pavement of the Strand that day, his mind may have been occupied with any of them. It may, of course, have been threshing out some problem of his own chartered accountant's business, although it is just as likely it was ruminating on the particular portion of Holy Scripture which he had been reading that morning. It is impossible to know what it was he had been thinking about before he met Dr Kenneth Buxton, on leave from his hospital work in Burundi, whom he met in the street that day. What history proves, however, is that during the course of the conversation that followed, his memory, like a well-trained secretary, turned up with the right item in the 'Awaiting Attention' file.

The medical missionary himself was glad of the opportunity to talk over with this accountant about whom he had heard, some of the business matters that were harassing him. He was perplexed about a number of things just then, was Dr Kenneth, of which legal business connected with finance was the least. Far more worrying was his uncertainty about his own future. After fifteen years in charge of the Ruanda Mission hospital in Burundi, with his wife at his side, he had brought her back to England with their children, knowing that she could not return to Africa with him. Not only was her own health being impaired, but the children were at the age when they must go to school in England. On top of that his mother-in-law, Grace Wakefield Bragg, was a widow now, and needed her daughter. The obvious thing was for Agnes to remain in England to make a home for the children and her mother, while he returned to Africa alone. This he had done.

He was back in England again now, to visit the family and to find the right answer to the question 'Is this the way I must continue – working alone in Africa, with a few weeks holiday at home once a year, leaving the family responsibilities all to Agnes? Or . . . ?'

He did not want to settle down in England. It was not only that the work in Burundi was deeply satisfying, and the fellowship between himself and the staff better than anything he had ever known before, that was holding him. He knew that the temptation to cling to a congenial situation can be as strong and insidious as that to get out of one that is disagreeable. In any case, the desire to be with his own family was equally powerful, and it was evident that he could no longer enjoy both at the same time.

The reason for his unwillingness to remain in England lay deeper than merely human reasons. As a young man he had given his life to God for service in Africa. Here was the crux of the matter. He did not want to withdraw in middle life. He wanted to finish the course. He had secretly rather despised some missionaries he had known who, for one reason or another, having committed themselves to work a lifetime in a certain country had failed to do so. He did not want to join their ranks, yet the disturbing conviction that he might have to do so was growing. This was what was lying uneasily in the secret recesses of his mind when, in the course of conversation, Mr Jacob suddenly asked him,

'Do you know any doctor who would be interested in the post of medical superintendent at the Mildmay Mission Hospital?'

It was not necessary for him to go into any explanations as to what and where the Mildmay was, for Kenneth Buxton had known about the mission hospital in London's East End from the time he was a small boy. The charming and dainty Miss Cattell had been matron there at the time, and came for her holidays to her home near where the Buxton family lived. She had regaled Kenneth and his sister Ruth with her descriptions of the place, and had so won Ruth's heart that she eventually took her nursing training there. Two cousins had been Council members at various times, and an aunt had been elected as one of the first two Mildmay representatives when the Group Management Committee met. Yes, he knew the Mildmay Mission Hospital, and Mr Jacob's question was like an unexpected green filter-light arrow pointing away from the road he had been travelling. That was a road on which the lights ahead seemed to have turned from green to amber – the Africa road.

'A doctor for the post of superintendent at the Mildmay?' He spoke cautiously. 'What qualifications are needed?'

Mr Jacob told him. 'A doctor at consultant status. A committed Christian. One who has served in missionary work overseas. One with experience in hospital administration.'

He asked for further particulars, and went on his way to continue with the programme of deputation meetings that had been planned for him – and to review the events of his life which had led him to this distracting period of uncertainty.

It was not the first time in his life that his spirit had been clouded by doubts. As a young medical student at Cambridge he had gone through the dim experience. He was applying himself more and more to his studies in medicine, with an increasing sense of inner desolation which he tried to ignore, until something someone said threw light on the situation. He had been studying his medical books diligently enough, but ignoring the Word of God. He ought to have known better, for even as a child he had heard often enough in his own home that 'man . . . lives by the Word of God'. And when, at a seaside beach mission, he had committed his life to Christ, it was the emphasis on 'the morning watch' alone with God, that had impressed him. He had no excuse for having neglected it, and felt ashamed of himself. Once he readjusted things, applying mind and will to reading the Bible and obeying its precepts, inward life was renewed and dreariness dissolved. It was probably that early experience that directed his attention to Bible study to an unusual degree, and later to the importance of Bible teaching.

The next unsettling period came when he was doing his houseman's year at St Thomas' Hospital. As leader of the Students Christian Union he became acquainted with Agnes Bragg, who was leader of the Nurses Christian Union, and all set to go to China as a missionary, like her parents before her. People were probably less surprised when the two got engaged than when they organised a missionary meeting in which their two Unions combined, thus bringing medical students down to the level of mere nurses! They met with some sharp opposition and criticism over that, for those were the days when professional class distinctions were very clearly defined. (Even at the Mildmay Mission Hospital the young house doctors refrained from conversation with the nurses, who stood back respectfully when they appeared in the wards. More than one ardent suitor had to declare his feelings from a telephone box outside the hospital after he went off duty!)

They expected their engagement to be of long duration, for the China Inland Mission at that time required its members to be for two years in China before they embarked on matrimony. China was the place to which they were going, and Agnes was already in the C.I.M. Women's Training Home at Highbury while he was completing his houseman's year at St Thomas', when something happened which threatened to shatter their plans and break their engagement.

They had gone together to a Buxton family gathering. A missionary minded family was that branch of the Buxtons, descendants of Sir Thomas Powell Buxton who worked with Wilberforce for the deliverance of slaves. One of them was Barclay Buxton of the Japan Evangelistic Band, and another was Alfred Buxton, son-in-law of C. T. Studd who founded the Worldwide Evangelisation Crusade. Alfred Buxton and his wife Edith were back in England after several years in Africa, and he was full of enthusiasm about what he saw as a strategic opportunity in Ethiopia. The Emperor had asked for his help in building and opening a medical school. It would be the first medical school in the country, and with an evangelical medical man in charge, what could not be accomplished for the furtherance of the Gospel and the good of the people!

Agnes noticed a gleam in Kenneth's eye she had never seen before as he listened to his cousin. And when Alfred looked directly at Kenneth and said,

'Wouldn't you be the man for this?' she almost caught her breath. It was as though a deep warning bell tolled in the distance, disturbing the tranquillity of her mind. Kenneth – Ethiopia?

She looked at him, and she knew.

'What will you do if God is calling Kenneth to Ethiopia?' murmured Edith. So Edith had sensed it, too! They were sitting side by side, and Agnes had no answer. She was feeling slightly stunned. But that very evening she and Kenneth faced up to the possibility that they were being called in opposite directions.

'We must each be sure of God's will,' they said, and agreed not to meet again until they had discovered His plan for their individual lives. Kenneth returned to his hospital duties and a deepening conviction, tinged with grief, that God had called him, not to China with Agnes, but to Africa . . ..

As for Agnes, she spent five miserable days thinking, praying and coming to no conclusion at all. Eventually she wandered into the library, picked up an old Bible that had belonged to Hudson Taylor, and turned the pages to the Psalms.

'Whom have I in heaven but Thee?' The words caught her eye, and then she noticed some words written beside them in ink that was faint with age.

'This verse spoke to me at a time when I was in great perplexity,' she read. Suddenly the famous pioneer of the Mission she expected to join seemed very near and very ordinary. He, too, had known perplexity! She looked again at the verse that had spoken to him, and it spoke to her, too. 'Whom have I in heaven but Thee?' Every human claim faded before the supremacy of the One Who had called her to follow Him. She took off her engagement ring and laid it on the verse, and whispered,

'Lord! Lord, I won't put this on again unless you show me you want me to go to Ethiopia with Kenneth. I love you best – I'll go to China without him if You say so.'

But He did not say so. The next morning she picked up her Bible to continue her daily reading. It was in the eighth chapter of Acts, and at the twenty-sixth verse she was arrested as suddenly as had been Philip the evangelist himself, by the words, 'Arise, and go toward the south. . . . '

The south - not the east! The significance of it, coming so clearly and unexpectedly after that simple but urgent prayer, could not fail to impress her. Africa was the southern continent, China was in the east. She read on, and again she started. 'Behold a man of Ethiopia. . . . '

That settled it, for with it came a steadying sense that God had spoken. Her uncertainty was at an end, and with it Kenneth's sense of grief. They married and in high expectation set off for Ethiopia, at once humbled and elated by the honour conferred upon Kenneth who, at the invitation of the Emperor, was to establish the first medical school in the country.

As it turned out, he never opened a medical school in Ethiopia. Instead, he and Agnes manned a Red Cross hospital, surrounded with dug-outs, and constantly alerted by air raid warnings. War had broken out, the Italians were invading Ethiopia, and eventually the Buxtons found themselves returning to England on the same ship as was carrying the Emperor into exile.

Kenneth felt rather battered. He had been so confident that God had ordained an overseas medical missionary career for him, and yet, what had he accomplished? The hospital he was to have built was but a dream. Although it was through no fault of his own that he was back from the mission field without a job and attached to no missionary society, he had to face the fact of his position. He did not know what to do. Various opportunities opened to him, but none of them evoked any response in his heart.

It was into this fog of uncertainty that light began to pierce with the invitation to go to another African country. Dr Stanley Smith of the Ruanda Mission put before the Buxtons the far reaching opportunities in Ruanda through medical work. Evangelism was being carried on there by African and western missions, but they were confronted by barriers of prejudice, paganism and witchcraft. A demonstration of the love of God through the healing arts among disease-ridden, impoverished people could melt those barriers.

Dr Stanley Smith explained that he had nothing to offer them in the way of influence or money. There was no emperor inviting them to open a hospital in the capital, nor a substantial bank balance on which they could draw. There was, in fact, about £5 in hand for the hospital waiting to be built! If they went to the task that was being suggested it would mean hardship and isolation, and many tests of faith. The only qualified staff members would be their two selves, though there would be African fellow workers eager to help and to learn.

Would they go?

It did not take them long to decide. 'Yes,' they said. 'It would be a privilege.'

The place to which they went was in open country, with grass six feet high, and the water supply a mile away. But there was a challenge about it, and moments of exultation as needs were met from various unexpected sources, like the ravens who fed Elijah. As for the hospital, it seemed to grow slowly but steadily out of the very ground. Clay bricks made on the spot were built up as walls – then rooms – then a house – then a hospital – then a nurses' training school. . . .

The Buxtons worked very hard.

The hospital must be the very best that Kenneth could make it, and the same went for Agnes where the nurses' training was concerned. There were times when the doctor sat down to a meal rather grim-faced, his wife absent-mindedly silent, the children uneasy. The problems of the hospital had a way of creeping in to rob life of its spontaneity and joy. Family relationships were somewhat strained on such occasions.

As a medical man Kenneth Buxton was a success. He was realising his boyhood ambition of building a mission hospital in a pioneer area, and gaining a reputation as a surgeon. Furthermore, he was doing a regular job of Bible teaching, for which he put in a lot of preparation. The studies he led were full of good, sound, evangelical theology

He was very busy. The Africans knew it. 'The Bwana doctor is like a signpost,' they said. 'When we go to see him he always points one way – to the door! He is too busy.'

She was very busy. 'The Bwana's wife gets on her bicycle and comes over and does many things,' the Africans on the staff observed. 'But she's too busy to stop and talk.'

It went on like that for a long time, but eventually Kenneth and Agnes were told what was being said. They felt ashamed, and were trying to rectify things, when they learned something else. Kenneth's Bible teaching was not wanted.

They were sitting in the drawing room, waiting for the African staff members to come for the weekly Bible study, when the door opened to admit three or four of them. Their shiny, dark-skinned faces looked grave, and they would not sit down.

'We've come to tell you we're not coming to the Bible study,' they said. Then they went on, gently, diffidently,

'We don't want your Bible teaching any more, Bwana.'

'Oh!' gasped Agnes.

'Why not?' asked Kenneth, trying to hide the sense of shock that was numbing him. He waited for their reply, and it came, very simply and quietly.

'We want more light.'

We want more light. The words sank in, quietly flooding in with all that they implied, though left unsaid. Those well-prepared Bible studies of his contained much knowledge, much learning, but they left the listeners uninspired. They did not come from deep, vivid, personal experience. He had to face the realisation that the fault lay in himself. Those Bible studies had become an end in themselves, the fulfilling of a missionary duty, rather than a revelation of the power of the risen, living Christ.

'We want more light,' his African staff members had said, and they stood waiting for his reply.

He might have been indignant.

He might have been offended.

He might have been stubborn, insisting that they needed the teaching.

But he and Agnes were both aware of the approach of Reality, and already a sense of awe was subduing them. Kenneth looked at those African fellow-believers of his, and said quietly,

'Thank you. Thank you for telling me.' They moved towards the door.

'Please pray for us,' he added. They smiled, quick, warm, African smiles, and went out.

The following day he and Agnes did not go to the hospital. They had agreed to spend the day alone, each in a different room, to hear what God the Lord would say. Something was wrong – with them. They must find out what it was.

Although it was the interview about the Bible studies that had brought matters to a head, they had both been conscious for some time that a vital, spiritual movement was at work, in which they had no part. They were in the heart of the area where the revival which became world-famous originated. They had seen for themselves the effects of it, seen lives aglow with love and joy, heard the uninhibited, fervent prayers, the warm, happy singing. Christians in other parts who heard about it spoke of 'the Ruanda revival', with its emphasis on love linked with complete openness and sincerity among fellow-believers. The Buxtons had seen it for themselves, had heard of the way erstwhile enemies had become friends, known of the 'fellowship meetings' where master and man, old and young sat together, tears of joy trickling quietly down their faces as they bowed in the presence of the invisible One who had been made flesh, and dwelt thus for a time among men. The atmosphere in homes and institutions and whole communities had been changed as wrongs had been righted, apologies made with contrition and received with humility, concealed crime confessed broken-heartedly. The Buxtons knew all about it, having seen it, yet secretly admitted to themselves that they knew nothing about it, not having experienced it. The revival, like the ocean around a rock, ebbed and flowed around the hospital, their hospital, but never seemed to flow in.

It had worried them. They talked it over together, decided to take a little time once a week to pray about it. Now they felt like employees who had been summoned to a private conversation with the Chief.

Hours later, just before nightfall, they came together again, to tell what they had learned. It was very simple, very basic, and as old as time.

'It's my pride,' said Kenneth in a low voice. 'Proud of myself . . . Proud of what I've achieved . . . Proud of my reputation as a surgeon. . . . '

'The Lord has shown me,' said Agnes with a little sob in her voice, 'He's shown me what I really am. Just a hard nursing sister – no love. I've been nursing for years, but . . . hard. No love. . . . Failing as a mother, too, at home. . . . '

But then she went on, 'It's the sense of His forgiveness, and the power in His blood to cleanse. . . . ' The hardness had been melted, and there was a new expression on her face, 'It fills me with gratitude.'

They knelt together, their faces moist with their tears, to pray.

After a time they rose to their feet and listened. In the distance they heard the muted sound of lilting song.

'It's the fellowship meeting,' they said. They had rarely been to a fellowship meeting. They had felt ill at ease with the spontaneous praying and singing and telling of experiences where Jesus had come to heal and to correct and to empower. A well conducted Bible study with Kenneth leading it and plenty of cross references to turn up to prove or emphasise some doctrine was the sort of gathering in which they had felt at home. But now they were drawn to that meeting.

'Let's go! Let's go and tell them what God has been saying to us,' they said, and went across the stubbly grass to stand in the open doorway, looking in on the sea of black, curly-haired heads that turned towards them enquiringly.

Perhaps they looked like two rather shy and wistful children as they stood there, the Bwana and his wife. Perhaps there was something unusually moving about the candour with which these two whose word was law in the hospital told of their meeting with the One who was Lord of all, and how He had pointed out what was wrong. Perhaps some of those present were reminded of their own dark, dark sins from which they had received the wonderful easing of forgiveness when they had confessed them as they came to Jesus Who had died on the cross for them. Whatever it was, the fellowship meeting seemed to open its arms to receive them in a tender, exultant embrace, and as the moon sailed slowly across the star-lit African sky they all prayed and they prayed and they prayed, and they sang and they sang and they sang.

That was the beginning of it, as far as the Buxtons were concerned. They had been left high and dry before, those ebbing and flowing waters of revival swirling around them but leaving them unrefreshed. 'Dry because high' was the phrase they often used later, laughing at themselves and those old, proud attitudes that had cut them off from their fellow-workers, western and African alike. It was some weeks before all the barriers had been swept away, but the Spirit of holiness and love was not to be denied now, and the time came when the Buxtons could report, 'We're experiencing a fellowship among members of the hospital staff, and in the home, that we've never known before.'

It seemed to reach from top to bottom. The smart young 'high class workers' who considered the menial jobs beneath them were now willing to roll up their sleeves even to clean the smelly ulcers on the patients' feet that were crawling with flies. The first time it happened the amazed ulcer patient burst into song, praising God!

There were confessions of dishonesty, too, and bribery, with restitution being made as stolen property was returned. In the wards the young nurses who had been willing to do only the minimum of what their duties demanded now took a personal interest in the patients, coming in during their free time to talk to them and help them. What perhaps touched Kenneth Buxton more than anything else was the change in the patients in the despised ulcer camp. Their bickering and discontent ceased, and one hot afternoon he looked across the compound to see a sight he never forgot. It was a string of them, limping on their poor bandaged feet, leaning on their sticks and singing as they straggled along a narrow rocky path to go to a nearby village and 'tell the people about Jesus'. It was something he saw many times during those wonderful years of spiritual blessing, and it rarely failed to bring a lump to his throat, and a moistness to his eyes.

The thought of leaving it all now was an unwelcome one. He wrote to friends in Africa, men whose judgement he respected, and asked what they thought about his remaining in England to apply for the post of Medical Superintendent of the Mildmay Mission Hospital in East London. They all advised him to do so. So he sent in his application, but he was still uneasy.

'I gave my life to Africa,' he said to a clergyman he met one day, and to whom he revealed something of the inner conflict that was troubling him. 'I gave my life to Africa, and I really have no peace about remaining in England, even though my family is here, and my African friends all advise me to do so.'

The clergyman looked at him sympathetically. 'I understand your feeling like that,' he said, 'But after all, you didn't give your life to Africa.'

The missionary looked at him enquiringly.

'You gave your life to Christ, didn't you? You gave your life to Christ – not to Africa.'

That simple sentence dissolved his confused thought like the morning sun dissolving mist. 'You gave your life to Christ, not to Africa.' It was not for him to decide how or where he would spend his days, what he would do with his life. He viewed his application for the job at the Mildmay differently after that. His Master had said, 'I am he that shutteth and no man openeth; and openeth and no man shutteth.' If the Government appointed him to the Mildmay Mission Hospital, he would accept that as being the way his Master wanted him to go. If God was working His purposes out through nations as well as through individuals, if He was indeed the God of history, then He was able to get Kenneth Buxton appointed to the Mildmay through Government now, as He would have been able to do it through the Mildmay House Committee in years gone by.

While he was waiting for the decision, he thought much about the aims of the hospital as outlined in the Trust Deed. How could the healing of the sick and the diffusing of simple Gospel truth be worked out in practice, increasingly, in a Christian hospital in the National Health Service?

The healing of the sick called for men and women skilled in their professions – but those whose qualifications put them in the top rank would scarcely be likely to respond to calls from a small East End hospital. Only a call from God would draw such consultants to the Mildmay. If God would do that! (It was something he was to see and marvel at in the years that lay ahead.)

But the healing of the sick was not to be confined to the patients in the mission hospital in London's East End. He remembered what he had seen in Africa, the poverty and the disease and the pain. He remembered how difficult he had found it to keep up with new trends and techniques in medicine when he was out there, running a mission hospital, and how he had sometimes longed for a few days intensive study that would bring him up to date. Refresher courses for missionary doctors might help to supply others with what he had lacked. It was a way in which the Mildmay could fulfil its aims further afield than Bethnal Green and Shoreditch!

One of the pleasures of going to the Mildmay, if he were appointed, would be to be the Superintendent of a mission hospital that was well equipped. Since the Government had taken over, there had been a steady improvement along the line of kitchen stoves and sink units, gas fittings and electric appliances, all with a view to the production of tastier, more hygienic and even more nourishing meals, and an easing of strain in the kitchen. There had even been talk about the building of an extension!

As for the other half of the hospital's aim, the diffusion of simple Gospel truth, his experience in Africa had taught him that 'the effectiveness of any mission hospital is in proportion to the depth of spiritual life in all the members of its staff'. It was not only ability to proclaim Gospel truth by lip that mattered, but the out-working of it in personal relationships and practical service, and the willingness to go 'the second mile'. He had learned something about that in Africa, and knew where the secret of it lay.

Lord, bend this proud and stiff-necked I
Help me to bend the neck and die,
Beholding Him on Calvary
Who bowed His head for me.

The words came to mind constantly, words he had sung so often in Africa. He would need them as much in a London hospital in the National Health Service as in a mission hospital in Burundi. The same principle must be applied in the new situation.

The more he thought about it, the more enthusiastic he became, so that it was almost with dismay he learned that things were not going smoothly with the Government, and that the Government wasn't too ready to appoint him. The set-back, as often happens, only served to strengthen his conviction that he was on the right road, and when at last the word came that his application had been accepted, all doubts about leaving Africa for England disappeared. He took up his new appointment on 1 October, 1954.

* * *

As it happened, May Ryan took up her appointment about the same time, as one of the hospital cleaners. She did not know much about the place, although she had been to the out-patients department once or twice, to take there the child she was looking after. She was working for a Roman Catholic family at the time, and being a Roman Catholic herself, had gone somewhat apprehensively. Her fears had been allayed by what she had seen and heard there, though she was not too happy about sitting through the service in the out-patients' department. 'We mustn't sing here – it's sin!' whispered her little charge anxiously. 'Ssh!' replied May in an undertone. 'They're going to heal your ear aren't they – so that's enough!' It was two or three years later that she found herself without a job and someone suggested the Mildmay, and she went along to see if they needed a daily cleaner. She little knew, as she went in the door that day that she was to find her life's fulfilment there.

Chapter Eleven

DEEP CALLS TO DEEP

May Ryan came to London in the 1930's, leaving the hills and the green fields of County Clare behind for ever, except in her memory, where they lived on along with her grandfather, and her gentle young husband, and their baby girl.

'God took them from me,' she said. 'He let me have them for a little time. But they died early - so I've been alone most of my life.' Her old grandfather's God-fearing example had precluded the self-pitying attitude that might have overcome her when sorrow piled on sorrow. The young widow found that even her hope of becoming a nurse had to be relinquished through ill health. That is how it came about that she responded to the suggestion of two friends that she should come over and try her luck in London.

She got a job as nurse-maid in a family, and when the family moved from Harrow to the East End, she moved, too. The mistress was kind to her fiery young Irish maid, and May had no complaints to make about the treatment she received. It was all right while she was busily employed, but eventually the children needed a nurse-maid no longer, and May became a 'daily' and got a little room for herself not far from Shoreditch Parish Church. When she had finished her work she would wander slowly round the churchyard, where at least there were some people sitting on the seats, and pigeons flopping heavily on to the ground, and sparrows twittering and hopping around. Living creatures.

'What's the matter with you, dearie?' asked a woman kindly one day. 'I see you here every day, walking around, and you're always crying.'

May, those large dark eyes of hers brimming with tears, answered simply,

'I'm lonely.'

The woman nodded sympathetically. She seemed to understand, and made a suggestion.

'Why don't you get a cat?'

'Get a cat?' asked May incredulously. 'A cat!'

Her thoughts went back to County Clare, and the cows with their slow contented munching; horses, too, whinneying around in their desire for human companionship. But cats!

'Get a cat? A cat couldn't talk to you,' she said.

'Well, the cat couldn't talk to you,' acknowledged the woman. 'But you could talk to the cat. It 'ud be company for you.' So May got a little cat, and after that she felt less lonely, with a living creature to think about, and buy fish for, and worry over if it didn't come home at night. The little cat, being a cat, adopted an indifferent attitude towards May's blandishments and confidences, but May was not discouraged. She knew it was only a pose. It was not the nature of cats to be demonstrative, to put themselves in a position where they might be rebuffed. Personal dignity must be maintained at whatever cost to personal inconvenience, and May knew that, if offended, her little cat would stalk away from the most tasty, fragrant, mouthwatering plate of fish she could contrive to produce, and withdraw to the roof in stately silence, deaf to her entreaties. Then it was a matter of waiting in humble contrition until the majestic little creature deigned to return. But it always did return, as May knew it would. Cats are like all living creatures – they know who loves them. May was certain of that.

As the years passed she became more and more of a cat-lover, shrewdly observing their individual tendencies. There were the cats that liked to sit on a wall, where everyone could see what they were doing, and admire them. There were the venturesome cats, and there were the cats whose fur stood on end if you so much as looked at them, and who hissed with a hate that sprang from fear. She was especially sorry for the little alley cats, easy prey for all the toms, who crawled on their distended bellies under the gates of factories from the shrieking of children who rushed after them. Her eyes blazed with such a righteous anger when she saw that happen that the children, suddenly made aware of her, melted away in silence.

'When a cat plays with a bird it's doing no wrong,' she said. 'Because it's the nature of the cat. It doesn't know any different. But when I see human beings tormenting something weaker – ah, then I get angry, because they've got something the animals haven't got. They've got a conscience. They know when they're doing something wrong. They *know*. . . . ' And if the children had managed to smother the protests of conscience in the absence of any other protests, May's blazing eyes and her forceful, deliberate, knife-edged declarations stabbed through to bring conscience to work again. That something the animals had not got stood in judgement of actions that ought never to have been allowed, and the culprits slunk away.

May had been in London for twenty years when she got her job at the Mildmay, and most of that time had been spent in the area around Shoreditch and Hoxton and Bow. She'd known the Mildmay from the outside all that time, listened for the chiming of the clock, but had never gone inside beyond the out-patients' department. Now it was different. Now she was one on the inside, with the right to go up the three flights of stairs and into the children's ward without any regard to the notice on the door about visiting hours. She had a right to go along to the kitchen premises, too, and down into the basement where the linen was kept, and the stocks of household goods. And before very long she found to her surprise she had the right to go into the mission hall when there were services on.

The Sister who had engaged her assured her of this. She had gone up to the children's ward to see how things were going on there, and seeking out May had asked her pleasantly,

'And are you getting on all right, Mrs Ryan?'

Now one of May's characteristics was that she gave expression to gratitude when she felt it, like the cat that purrs when it is pleased, and she was feeling very grateful for the job at Mildmay. She did not regret having walked out on the cafe proprietress who had taken advantage of her good nature in offering to do a share of the work of another employee who had gone off sick. The understanding had been that she should do part of the work, and the proprietress a part, but when it came to it, May found herself left to do the lot. She flared up immediately she realised what was happening. She'd do anything for anybody, would May, but she wasn't going to be put on! She gave the proprietress a piece of her mind, along with her notice, which was to take effect then and there. It had meant visiting the Labour Exchange later to which she was not accustomed, and which she did not like, so she was very glad indeed to be on a self-respecting basis again, earning her own living. She was grateful, and in response to the Sister's enquiry she said, 'It's very well I'm getting on'. Then, looking her straight in the eyes, she added,

'And it's thanking you I am for giving me the job.'

The Sister smiled. 'Oh, I don't think I'll regret it,' she said, and as far as May's work was concerned she never had cause to do so. (When she heard, from time to time, of angry altercations in which the new daily cleaner was involved, it may have been another matter. Mrs Ryan was no respecter of persons, and liable to express herself in unexpected ways, as one of the nurses discovered. She had been hurrying along the corridor, and had shoo-ed the hospital cat, and the next moment found herself precipitated head on into the laundry basket by a furious shove from the back.)

'Mrs Ryan, we have a little prayer meeting in the mission hall every morning,' the Sister went on. 'We'd like it very much if you could come and join us.'

May paused a moment. She felt she would very much like to attend that prayer meeting – whatever a prayer meeting was! But she could not go under false cover.

'I'd like to,' she said. 'But there's something I think you ought to know. I'm of a different faith to you. I'm a Roman Catholic.'

'Oh, that doesn't matter,' replied Sister without hesitation. 'You'll be all the more welcome if you come along. We'd be glad to have you come.'

So May, who was an independent thinker and not one to be over-awed by what the Reverend Father might say or think about a member of his flock straying into Protestant circles, went along. It was all very different from the sort of thing she was accustomed to. People talked to God as though they knew Him! They shut their eyes and bowed their heads, but apart from that they talked to Him as freely as if he were – well, an employer whom they respected very much, and in whose consideration for them they had the utmost confidence, as they thanked Him for His goodness and told Him of their difficulties, and asked

Him for His help.

May was drawn by it all – the praying and the singing and the reading of little bits from the Bible, and by the friendly atmosphere, and the kindness. She told Maude about it. 'The kindness – it's like velvetty down my skin,' she said. 'Some of the people there. . . . They're so busy, and they work so hard, but they've always got time to stop and have a word with you. It's interested in you they are. . . .'

Maude was the manageress of a small button factory, and her great friend. Maude was as placid as May was impulsive, and she listened often and long as May talked about the Mildmay. Then one day she said,

'You're always talking about that hospital. Anyone would think it was Heaven!'

'If you were there, you'd know what I mean,' said May. She herself had not been there long before she decided that as far as religion was concerned, she was going the Mildmay way. 'I've changed my denomination,' she said firmly to the Roman Catholic priest who came to her door one day. 'I'm a Baptist now.' It was the only Protestant denomination she could think of on the spur of the moment. 'So I'll say to you – Good day!' and closed the door.

She got into the way of going to work early, unconsciously absorbing the atmosphere of the place, the peace, the awareness of a Presence. She did not want to rush into her day's work. It was good just to pad along the corridor after she had changed into slippers, and look into the mission hall, and maybe have a chat with one of the Sisters. Her quick eyes noted when they looked tired or strained, and sometimes, with that Irish sixth sense of hers perceiving the cause, she would slip back into the mission hall and sit down quietly to pray before going to get her bucket and broom, and start on her vigorous cleaning.

One morning there was an unusually anxious expression on a Sister's face. She had to attend a committee meeting that morning at which decisions would be made which might affect the evangelical character of the hospital, and she was uncertain of her ability to say the right thing at the right time. May would not have understood the intricacies of the situation even if the Sister had been free to explain them to her, which, of course, she was not. She looked into May's earnest face, and asked her to pray that everything would work out for God's glory at that committee meeting. Then she went on her way.

But May could not go on hers. A sense of foreboding settled on her spirit, as though invisible, unseen forces were closing in, menacing and dark. The men and women who sat around the committee table that morning were merely bent on doing their duty, on making suggestions and decisions that would be in the best interests of the causes they represented. The little Irishwoman cleaner, however, polishing the brass taps over the sink, saw something else. The enemy was approaching. It was not a flesh and blood affair, not the members of the committee that she saw, or she would readily have gone into the attack, broom and bucket and all! But what she sensed was not human conflict. It was more like what the old hymn described,

'Christian, dost thou see them
On the holy ground?
How the hosts of Midian
Prowl and prowl around. . . .'

and May, like a settler defending his homestead against the Indians silently approaching through the undergrowth, felt desperately the need of another gun.

She went in search of Zachariah.

Zachariah was a big tall African, and he had come to

England and the Mildmay to learn dispensing. May had a high regard for him, with his exuberant faith in God, and his sincerity, and his uninhibited way of praying. Zachariah would understand.

By the time she got to the dispensary her sombre eyes were burning like coals.

'Zachariah,' she said. He looked at her, and his face grew solemn. Mrs Ryan was disturbed. What was it?

'Zachariah!' She spoke in short staccato sentences. 'They're trying to push God out of this hospital!' She paused a moment, then went on,

'It says in the Bible that where two or three are gathered together, He's there. Will you come and pray with me? Pray about that committee meeting?'

Zachariah knew even less about what was on the agenda for that committee meeting than did May, but that did not matter. Her sense of urgency had communicated itself to him. He nodded.

'We'll go to the mission hall,' said May, and led the way along the passage.

She never forgot the way Zachariah prayed that day. He knew something of the history of the Mildmay, saw evidence of the dedicated lives that had gone to the building of it, and almost with sobs he pleaded,

'Oh, God! Preserve this little hospital – this little hospital that's been run on pennies and sacrifice!'

They stood together, the tall African in his white overall and the little Irishwoman with her feet in carpet slippers and her head in a scarf, for only a few minutes, heads bowed, then went back to their tasks.

A few hours later Sister came walking briskly in through the front gates, caught sight of May, and waved to her, smiling. She looked relieved.

'It's all right!' she called as she hurried on.

May pursed her lips, nodded slowly, then made sure the hospital cat had plenty to eat, and went home.

* * *

The smallness of the Mildmay was still one of its major problems. Only fifty-four beds! The casualty department was kept busy day and night, and the mission hall, also doing duty as the out-patients' waiting room, saw a steady flow of people coming in. But the physiotherapy and X-ray departments were bursting at the seams, the records' department was little more than a cupboard in the wall, and as for the wards themselves, fresh curtains and new equipment could not disguise the fact that according to modern standards they were inadequate, with no single rooms in which to put patients who were needing special treatment, and kitchens that were barely big enough for a nurse to turn round. The nurses' home was too small, while the accommodation for the Sisters remained unchanged from the days when Matron Cattell had reigned.

The hospital had escaped the official axe so far, but how long could it continue to live if it ceased to grow? Unless an extension were added, there would be the danger of its being proved too uneconomic for the National Health Service to be justified in keeping it open.

The closing down, by Government order, of another of the Mildmay institutions, the Memorial Hospital in Newington Green, North London, was the event which provided the unlikely solution to the Mission Hospital's problem. The vigilant guardians of the Mildmay interests observed what was happening, and while they had no power to prolong the life of the Memorial Hospital, and recognised the Government's right to close a hospital that had become redundant, they exerted their own right to enquire what would happen to the money the property would fetch. That money, they pointed out, had been given for a specific purpose, and in a democratic country could not be annexed out of hand. The money with which the Memorial Hospital had been built had been donated for the same sort of purpose as that of the Mission Hospital.

The outcome of the matter was that it was agreed the money should be allocated to the Mildmay Mission Hospital, and with that in hand the Mildmay was emboldened to ask for an extension to be built. Lord Stonham's impassioned plea about 'this little hospital that patients want to come to – some from the ends of the earth! This little hospital that has a waiting list for nurses, and that has already provided a considerable sum towards the cost of its own extension!' won the day when the reasonableness of the request was disputed. After many committee meetings, and much studying of estimates, and painstaking applications for planning permission, and all the things that make work, though not news, the day came when the foundation stone was laid, a simple ceremony which held at bay the builders' lorries, and the bricks and the cranes that were waiting to swoop in and take possession as soon as it was over.

That was in 1964, and a year of emotional upheavals it proved to be. It was not so much the inevitable inconvenience caused by the building of the extension that affected the staff, as the things that happened to some of the people they knew and loved.

It started with George Woodall, the hospital evangelist, being admitted to the men's ward as a patient. He became so critically ill that he was on the danger list. Again and again there was a subdued hush when in reply to the question 'How's Uncle George?' the answer was that he was still very ill. The time came when the medical staff knew that it was beyond human skill to save him, and could only stand by to see what God would do.

'Uncle George' as he came to be known, was the first full-time evangelist in the hospital, and his appointment had been a direct outcome of the transference of the hospital to the National Health Service. The National Health Service would see to the fulfilment of the aim, embodied in the Trust Deed, to heal the sick, but not to that of diffusing simple Gospel truth. The diffusion of simple Gospel truth was not its responsibility. As Mr Alexis Jacob saw things, it was the League of Friends that should occupy itself more specifically with that clause. So, as Chairman of the League, he approached the London City Mission to see if one of its hundred or so missioners could be appointed as a full-time worker in the Mildmay Mission Hospital, which was interdenominational in character, and was situated in just the sort of area where the L.C.M. thrived.

The London City Mission had just the man for the job, and as soon became evident, the Mildmay Mission Hospital had just the job for the man. George Woodall, tall, well-built, apparently strong and healthy man that he was, nevertheless had a physical condition which sometimes doubled him up with pain. He had suffered from colitis for years, though no one would have guessed it seeing him standing on a box at Hyde Park Corner or at the races, playing his accordion and singing hymns, dark eyes flashing and face aglow. The other members of those preaching bands were very glad when George was around. George had once been in the Grenadier Guards, and his unconscious air of confidence, his height, and the evident strength of his limbs had a surprising effect on hecklers. One look at him was sufficient to silence their quips, and after a minute or two they would quietly take themselves off.

At one time George thought he would like to be a missionary in Africa, but

'The Lord sent me to the gas-works at Fulham instead!' he would say with a grin. Fulham was his first appointment after joining the London City Mission, though he was sent to several other places after that – Ealing, Dagenham, Hoxton, Islington. But all the time he was battling with that painful and embarrassing complaint, and the opening at the Mildmay Mission Hospital seemed providential, for it would mean he would not have to be out in all weathers, and help would be on hand if he were ill.

He had won his way into hearts, with his ready smile that brought deep creases down his cheeks, and his way of sensing when people were feeling discouraged, or troubled, or sad. 'I'm here if you want me,' he seemed to say, as he walked quietly by, not intruding, but obviously ready to listen if needed. 'That's what Jesus is like,' he explained to one of the young stenographers who noticed that on days when she was depressed Uncle George would be sure to pass slowly past her office door and glance in with a little questioning smile. 'He doesn't force Himself on you, but He's there – ready to listen and ready to help if you ask Him to.'

And his hands! Those hands of Uncle George's that could twinkle over the keys of the piano and fill the room with melodies and trills, triumphant chords and soaring sound! Those hands that could dash off sketches of stars and angels, and stimulate or subdue the hospital choir!

But now Uncle George was lying in the men's ward, the curtains drawn around his bed, the nurses instinctively tip-toe-ing as they went in to look at him, the doctors shaking their heads as they studied his charts. 'Only a miracle will save him now,' they agreed. They waited and watched and prayed.

A miracle happened that time. It was no new thing, for it had happened before, and it happened again. In the most hopeless cases the doctors and nurses always knew that a miracle might happen, and in Uncle George's case it did. He recovered, and the sun shone again for the Mildmay!

Later on in the year, however, clouds appeared again, for it was in 1964 that the political turmoil in the Congo came to a head, and the Simba rising burst out in all its ugliness and cruelty.

Ever since 1960, when Belgium granted independence to the Congo, trouble had been brewing, with Prime Ministers following each other in quick succession endeavouring to make a nation out of peoples unprepared for the reponsibilities of citizenship. In 1963 the National Liberation Committee, as the rebel group called itself, set up its headquarters in Brazzaville. Prime Minister Tshombe's efforts at conciliation failed, and the rebels advanced. News filtered through of mass executions, with children organised as 'the Jeunesse' playing dance records as they watched. Then it was reported the white people were being held as hostages. The daring exploits of the mercenary army, mainly composed of white men, who plunged deep into rebel territory to deliver the captives, made headline news in the daily papers. Embassies and consulates, and the offices of missionary societies with workers in the Congo, were besieged by people wanting to know what was happening to their relatives or friends.

The first throb of real alarm that alerted the Mildmay was when someone heard that Elsie was in the danger zone. A brown-haired damsel of mischievous disposition, with a twinkle in her eye, was Elsie, and no one blamed young Doctor Harris, who came for two or three weeks as a locum, for falling in love with her – when they knew that was what had happened. At first the other nurses had been surprised at the abrupt way he pushed her aside when she wanted to help with a patient, refusing to let her assist him. 'Why is he so mean to Elsie?' they murmured, rather resentfully. 'She's done nothing wrong!' However, when they learned that he had pushed her aside because he liked her so much that her presence had a disturbing effect on his professional attitude, they smiled and forgave him. So Dr Harris had married Elsie Sexton and carried her off to do missionary work with him in the Congo.

And now – were they among those who were being cut off by the rebels? Would the jungle swallow them up?

As it happened the alarm concerning the Harris family proved to be needless. They were nowhere near the danger zone. It was a different matter where the Sharpes were concerned. Dr Ian Sharpe had done his houseman's year at the Mildmay, and while there had fallen in love with Staff Nurse Audrey Gibson. They were on the Congo list of Mildmay missionaries now, and with their three children were reported to be behind the rebel lines. Nothing more was known about them.

If there was no news of the Sharpe family, however, there was news about Dr Helen Roseveare, another Mildmay houseman, and it was almost worse than no news at all.

'Dr Roseveare's in the hands of the rebels!' It was weeks later, weeks of uncertainty when horrible apprehensions alternated between assurance that God would answer prayer, that news came through, to bring an excited cry of relief.

'Dr Roseveare! The mercenaries got through! She's safe!' It was one of the epics of the whole tragic period, the way the dare-devil mercenaries got through to deliver the little band of helpless women and children in the nick of time. Dr Roseveare was being flown home, along with others who had suffered with her, and who also needed hospital treatment. Could the Mildmay take them in?

Could the Mildmay take them in . . . !

When they arrived, calm and smiling, but looking 'as though they've aged a thousand years!' the Mildmay was stunned into silence. But at the prayer meetings voices were trembling with emotion as they pleaded for the protection of the others they knew – Margaret Hayes, the Sharpes and especially their three children. 'Lord! Don't let those little children be separated from their parents. Don't let them fall into the hands of cruel men!'

After months of silence authentic news came through at last. It was not what they had hoped for, but when they recovered from the shock they were able to thank God that there would be no separation in the Sharpe family. Father, mother and children had died together. And when Margaret Hayes, long since reported missing, feared dead, walked out of the jungle with her amazing stories of endurance and deliverances, the Mildmay bowed its head and worshipped.

The staff usually exchanged presents among themselves at Christmas time, but this year they felt they could not do it. They decided to pool the money instead, and send it to the Congo. It helped, just a little, to relieve their feelings.

* * *

Meanwhile, the building of the new extension to the hospital was creating a lot of dust, and the noise of lorries being driven over rough ground, of electric drills and clanging girders, was interspersed by ominous silences which indicated that for one reason or another the work had come to a standstill. But the time came at last, in 1965, when the builders' lorries all pulled out, leaving the new extension exposed to view with its glass entrance, its wide corridors, its open wards and its enlarged records and X-ray and casualty departments. It was ready for the opening ceremony. Her Royal Highness, Princess Alexandra arrived along the narrow cobbled alley by which Queen Mary in her carriage had approached it, but swept out over the wide new drive that led to the Hackney Road. The hospital had a new entrance, and what for nearly a century had been the main entrance now became the back door.

Percy, as Head Porter, had seen to it that everything was spick and span, and fit for the grand-daughter of a Queen. He was among those who were presented to the popular young Princess (as was Charlie Haynes, who happened to be a patient in Mathieson ward at the time), with his record of nearly half a century serving in the Mildmay.

Three years later Percy, too, was a patient in Mathieson ward. He had been there before, and to everyone's delight had made an almost miraculous recovery. This time, however, it was different.

'I'm going – going to be with the Lord,' he said. 'I want to go – to be with Him.' But there was a message he wanted to give before he left. He had a message for all 'the Mildmays', the little student nurses who had done their training there, the young doctors who had done their houseman's year in the East End mission hospital, and gone out, so many of them, to remote places with names that he could not pronounce. He thought about them, and wanted to send a message to them. It was put in the magazine and appeared after he died, and somchow it brought a quick, stinging sensation behind the eyes of those who read it. It was very simple.

'Tell them Percy sends his love to all "the Mildmays", and says goodbye.'

Chapter Twelve

A BRANCH OVER THE WALL

The group of people who had once been the governing body of the Mildmay Mission Hospital, and who were now merely the executive committee of the League of Friends, were faced with a problem. They sat round the table, listened to the financial report, and exchanged glances with brows upraised. The subject of money was one which had often occupied them in the past, and now here it was cropping up again, but in an entirely new guise. Whereas, in days gone by, the problems faced were usually to do with a shortage of money, the problem now was an excess of it. There was something like £7,000 in hand, and no apparent way of using it.

'We can't seem to stop people from sending money to the League,' said someone. 'Don't they realise the hospital has been taken over by the Government, and that we're not running it any longer?'

'I've told them, time and time again,' said the Secretary. 'It's all been explained in the magazine.'

'It's not right to keep the money doing nothing,' said someone else. 'Can't it be given to some good cause?'

'The League of Friends *is* the good cause! . . .'

'There must be a purpose for it. God must have some reason for sending it to us.'

The almoner made a suggestion, rather differently. 'There is a great need for convalescent homes in the country,' she said. 'So many of the patients really need a period of convalescence before returning to their homes.

But I can't always find one suitable for our patients – and their pockets! If only we had one of our own. . . .'

A convalescent home. A Mildmay convalescent home. The executive committee of the League of Friends brightened perceptibly. The idea was sown in fruitful soil, and Mr Alexis Jacob, as Chairman, sensed the feeling of the meeting.

He liked it when they were all of one mind. In fact, he usually refused to go forward until they were. 'We must stop!' he would say bringing long discussions not devoid of argument to an abrupt conclusion. 'Every resolution must be unanimous in the sight of God. Let us stop, and all pray.' After a short silence, when all heads bowed, there was no more difficulty, and decisions were then taken to the satisfaction of all.

The suggestion of a convalescent home evoked little enough argument – it appealed to all, and before long they were looking about for a suitable property. A house in Ramsgate was found, furniture and equipment were provided, and the opening date fixed.

It was at this point that things began to go awry. Who was to be the matron? Sister Muriel had been approached but had said no. She did not feel she should leave the fruitful spiritual field of the Mathieson Ward. Then the one whose appointment was all but settled said she could not leave the job she was in until a month later. She would be failing her colleagues in her present position if she did so. Couldn't the opening date be postponed one month? But the opening date had been fixed, and patients booked in. The committee, in a dilemma, appointed someone else, and the convalescent home was duly opened on the advertised date.

Three months later the committee of the League of Friends was looking for a new matron. The one it had appointed was leaving!

For Sister Muriel the news was disquieting, and when the League of Friends again approached her about taking over as matron of the convalescent home, she realised she must reconsider the matter. Then it began to dawn on her that the real reason for deciding not to leave the Mildmay had been because she loved the work there so much, she did not want to leave. What had appeared to be her duty had been merely her own desire! Once that became plain, and she was on her knees before God about it, there were no further problems. A delighted League of Friends' committee duly appointed her to the convalescent home, she resigned from the National Health Service since she was once more working for a voluntary organisation, and all was well.

Mr Alexis Jacob was gratified, but he soon became unsatisfied. The convalescent home was too small. Hospital social workers were making applications for patients to be admitted, and since the Mildmay claims naturally took precedence, there were many times when those applications had to be refused. The beneficial influences of the convalescent home where healing was extended to soul as well as body ought not to be limited to a handful of people, he decided, and the League of Friends' committee agreed with him. But while the convalescent home at Ramsgate was paying its way and posing no major financial problems, there was nothing in hand with which to so much as consider buying a larger property.

To Mr Alexis Jacob, however, this was not an insuperable obstacle. If God were with him in this matter, then He would provide what they needed, of that he was sure. By faith, prayer and keeping their wits about them, they would discover where that provision was. He had seen it happen before, and it would happen again.

And it did. The provision was, so to speak, on the doorstep – Mr Alexis Jacob's doorstep.

Within a stone's throw of his accountant's firm was a group of men in process of winding up the Zachery Merton Trust funds. Zachery Merton was a millionaire who died early in the twentieth century, and left a fortune to charity. Many were the organisations that had benefited by it, over the years, but at last the money was coming to an end. There remained a small sum, only £20,000 or so, to be disposed of, and that money had to be disposed of in a certain way. It could not go to orphanages or hospitals, schools or training centres, rehabilitation refuges for ex-prisoners or homes for the aged. It had been allocated for use in another way. It was to be used for convalescent homes.

Therefore the trustees of the Zachery Merton funds were looking for a suitable convalescent home project into which to channel the money. They invited applications which outlined clearly the plans that would be set in motion if only there were the money required. Mr Alexis Jacob's application on behalf of the Mildmay convalescent home was the one that was chosen.

All that now remained was to find a suitable property by the sea, with sufficient land around it to allow for an extension to be built if it became necessary to do so (it did). A small private hotel in Wordsworth Road, Worthing, was up for sale, duly inspected and surveyed, and pronounced eminently suitable for conversion into a convalescent home.

Mr Alexis Jacob was delighted. He strolled along the quiet, residential road and decided that the location was ideal for people recovering from operations or serious illnesses – no hills to climb, only a few hundred yards from the sea front, and near the shops! This was undoubtedly the place for the new Mildmay Convalescent Home to be established. The appropriate wheels were set in motion, plans were submitted for alterations, agreements signed with agents, the Ramsgate home put up for sale, and every prospect was bright. The opening took place in 1960, with the League of Friends of the Mildmay Mission Hospital glowing with satisfaction, and Matron Muriel Jameson tripping it out smartly as she showed guests around the place, all clean and fresh as it was, and fragrant with flowers.

Mr Alexis Jacob, however, was nowhere to be seen. One Bank holiday in the previous year he had been at a family gathering, and some of his younger relatives wanted to play tennis. They needed someone to make up the set, and called to Uncle Alexis to join them. Uncle Alexis, for all his 70-odd years, was good for a game, and grasping his tennis racket jumped cheerfully out through the drawing room window, and started to sprint for the court.

But he did not reach it. He suddenly staggered, and clutched his chest. . . .

For some whose Christian faith has triumphed buoyantly in the adversities of this mortal life, the traversing of the valley where death's shadow falls is a long, weary journey. They find the last lap of the pilgrimage fraught with many a secret struggle and horrible encounter. For Mr Alexis Jacob, however, it was otherwise. He took it, so to speak, at the double. 'He died very suddenly, of a heart attack,' people said. But those who knew him best, and knew where his heart had been all these years, did not think of it like that. The crumpled, lifeless body showed that at last he had made his exodus, and had really entered in.

EPILOGUE

'Excuse me, Miss Thompson!' The junior houseman's head appeared round the door of the room where I sat typing. 'Excuse me – but have you finished writing that book yet?'

I admitted I had not. How does one finish writing about something that is still going on?

'Then may I tell you about the man who was dying in Mathieson ward?' he asked eagerly. I indicated a chair, he sat down, and went on,

'He came into hospital in late December, 1971, with acute bronchitis and heart failure. Man in his sixties. He didn't respond to treatment, then began sinking very fast one Saturday early in January. I was in and out of the ward most of the day, and so were his relatives. No one thought he would live.'

About 6.15 the young houseman went off to the canteen, having done everything for the man that he could think of. 'I'll bet there will be an emergency call,' he thought to himself, rather heavily. He pictured himself dashing up the stairs in response to a call on his bleep, looking down at a lifeless form, speaking to the relatives. . . . However, the call did not come, and when he went up to the ward half an hour later, to his surprise the patient looked slightly better. At 7 p.m. it was seen that his pulse and respiration rates had taken a distinct turn in the right direction.

Early the following morning the night Sister said, 'You know, doctor, I think there must have been a miracle in the case of that patient. He's not going to die now, after all.'

And he didn't. He rallied so strongly and steadily that a couple of weeks later he was discharged, and walked out of the hospital.

What impressed the incident so deeply on the mind of the young houseman, however, was a conversation he had with someone on the other side of London two or three days after the patient had started to recover. As they were chatting his friend suddenly said,

'By the way, did you have a man who was dying in your hospital last Saturday evening at five and twenty minutes to seven? We were just sitting down to our evening meal, and I had the feeling that there was a man dying in the Mildmay Mission Hospital. I had the feeling so deeply that I told the others about it. I knew it was the Holy Spirit urging me. We all prayed for him – didn't know who he was, but we prayed. . . .'

The young houseman paused in his narrative, and looked at me. 'That was at 6.35, just the time I was sitting in the canteen expecting the emergency call,' he said.

'Amazing!' I breathed.

Then he indicated he had something else to tell. This was about a woman who had been brought into the hospital in a very bad state of acute, aggressive anxiety. So aggressive had she been that she had attacked him (embarrassing, to have to struggle with a woman in her night clothes!) and so anxious that she had tried to throw herself out of the window. Eventually they had to get her taken off to a psychiatric unit.

About a week later she phoned the young houseman at the Mildmay. She wanted to apologise for what she had been told she had done while she was there. She herself could remember nothing, except the text she had seen over her bed.

'Lying in the other hospital, I remembered that text. "I will rejoice over them to do them good", it was. The Lord used it to set my mind at rest. When the psychiatrist came to see me next time, he said, 'You're perfectly all right now. You can go home.'

There is always something like that happening at the Mildmay. It makes you realise that as well as the doctors and the nurses, and all the other members of the staff, Someone else is there.

* * *

Not only on the wards has that invisible Presence exercised an inexplicable control, either. In committee meetings when Government officials, bent on economising, have axed one after another of the smaller hospitals in the inner city, the Mildmay has escaped. It's different somehow, they have agreed. It ought to remain, even if it functions in a different way.

Of couse. The Mildmay is no bronze statue, unable to change with the times and adapt to current needs. Sitting at lunch with Dr Jim Walker in the hospital canteen one day late in 1981, I asked him how he saw the future of Mildmay.

'There are many handicapped people in East London,' he told me. 'Their lives are very restricted, often made much worse by small illnesses for which they would not be sent to a teaching hospital. Yet they need hospital care – could Mildmay not be the place to which they should come? I'm sure God had a plan for a change in the role of this hospital away back in the sixties with the new addition to wards, new outpatients department, new accident department. Perhaps this is the path He now wants us to consider. Meanwhile, the work of treating people as individuals who may have a spiritual need as well as a physical one goes on. . . . That's what we're here for.'

CHRONOLOGY

1866 Two Mildmay deaconesses go to Bethnal Green, where cholera has broken out.
1871 New Deaconess home opened. Miss Coventry in charge.
1872 First Mildmay Trust, incorporating 'diffusion of simple Gospel truth'.
1873 William Pennefather dies. Memorial fund for hospital opened.
1877 Warehouse in Turville Square converted into a 30-bed hospital.
1880 Dr William Gauld, returned from missionary work in China, becomes first Medical Superintendent.
1883 Mildmay starts training nurses.
1886 Fund opened for new hospital building.
1890 Foundation stone of new hospital laid in Austin Street, near Shoreditch Parish Church, by Lady Tankerville.
1892 New hospital opened, with 50 beds.
1913 Dr Gauld retires.
1914 First World War breaks out.
1917 Mildmay Conference Centre and Deaconess Home closed.
1919 Miss Dora Woodhouse appointed matron of the Mildmay Mission Hospital.
Miss Hancock joins as Enquiry Officer (forerunner of the Medical Social Worker).
1922 Dr Henry White, returned from missionary work in Persia, appointed Medical Superintendent of the Mildmay Mission Hospital.
State Registration of nurses instituted.
Mildmay recognised as a Nurses Training School.
1927 Mr Alexis Jacob joins Executive Committee.
1938 Out-patients extension opened by Queen Mary.
Sir George Hume, Chairman of the London County Council, becomes Chairman of the Mildmay Mission Hospital.

1939 Outbreak of Second World War.
Dr A.J. Watson, returned from missionary work in China, appointed Medical Superintendent.

1941 Annie McCall Hospital incorporated with the Mildmay Mission Hospital.

1943 Aims of hospital (to heal the sick and diffuse simple Gospel truth) incorporated in Trust Deed.

1945 Sir George Hume calls for special prayer after Government Commission reports that hospitals with less than 200 beds are uneconomic.

1946 Health Services Act passed.
Mildmay Mission Hospital continues as Nurses Training School in association with The London Hospital.

1948 Health Services Act comes into operation. Mildmay Mission Hospital's aims 'to heal the sick and diffuse simple Gospel truth' recognised in view of Clause 61 of the National Health Service Act.
Formation of the League of Friends of the Mildmay Mission Hospital.

1954 Dr Kenneth Buxton, returned from missionary service in Africa, appointed as Medical Superintendent.

1956 Mildmay Convalescent Home opened in Ramsgate – property of the League of Friends of the Mildmay Mission Hospital. Closed 1959.

1960 Mildmay Convalescent Home re-opened in Worthing.

1965 New extension of the Mildmay Mission Hospital, which now has 72 beds, opened by Princess Alexandra.

1971 Lady Missionar's post continues.

1974 Re-organisation of the National Health Service.
Appointment of Senior Medical Officer (Mr J.M. Walker, formerly with Rwuanda Mission). Social Work taken over by Tower Hamlets Borough from District Health Authority.
Sir Graham Rowlandson House for Nurses and Doctors opened. Wards upgraded.
Member of League of Friends Council appointed to serve on Tower Hamlets Community Health Council. Mildmay Mission Hospital Advisory Council inaugurated.

1977 Jacob Home for Nurses opened.

1979 Hospital Chaplain's post continues (L.C.M. Missioner).
Child Health Clinic moved into Out Patient Department.